P9-DTX-550

Text and Quality

Text and Quality

Studies of Educational Texts

Edited by
Peder Skyum-Nielsen

SCANDINAVIAN
UNIVERSITY PRESS

OSLO, COPENHAGEN, STOCKHOLM, BOSTON

Text and Quality
Peder Skyum-Nielsen (ed.)

© Scandinavian University Press (Universitetsforlaget AS) 1995, on license from Akademisk Forlag A/S (Academic Press · Copenhagen)

ISBN 82-00-22453-8

All rights reserved. No part of this publication may be reproduced, stored in a retrieval system, or transmitted, in any form or by any means, electronic, mechanical, photocopying, recording, or otherwise, without the prior permission of Scandinavian University Press. Enquiries should be sent to the Rights Department, Scandinavian University Press, Oslo, at the address below.

Typesetting: Akademisk Forlag A/S, Copenhagen
Printing: Reproset I/S, Copenhagen
Cover: Ib Spang Olsen
Copy-editing: Marianne Moring
The English text was prepared by Marlene R. Hansen

Printed in Denmark 1995

Oslo office
Scandinavian University Press
(Universitetsforlaget AS)
P.O. Box 2959 Tøyen,
N-0608 Oslo, Norway
Fax +47 22 57 53 53

Copenhagen office
Scandinavian University Press A/S
P.O. Box 54,
DK-1002 København K,
Denmark
Fax +45 33 32 05 70

Stockholm office
SCUP
Scandinavian University Press
P.O. Box 3255,
S-103 65 Stockholm, Sweden
Fax +46 8 20 99 82

Boston office
Scandinavian University Press
North America
875-81 Massachusetts Avenue
Cambridge MA 02139, USA
Fax +1 617 354 68 75

Contents

Introduction

What is meant by a "good" educational text, in this final decade of the 20th century?
Many interest groups have a stake in this topic: educational, economic, cultural and political. And a combination of viewpoints is needed if the question is to be answered fully and satisfactorily.

Eighteen Danish scholars have therefore got together to define the qualities of "good" educational texts today. From 1992-94 they have held meetings every month and discussed the different aspects of their common venture from various points of view.

Whilst working on this fundamental question of **educational rhetoric**, the group has benefited from the inspiring work of many outside investigators. Special mention should be made of the Norwegian textbook researcher Egil Børre Johnsen and the Swedish educationalist Staffan Selander. Both are internationally acclaimed for their work in the field of educational textual research, and together with the Danish group they have contributed to the present essay collection, *Text and Quality*.

It has been a fruitful and instructive experience for the group members to exchange notes concerning "the good educational text today", not least because between us we have been able to mobilise a large number of criteria and parametres of relevance within modern educational and rhetorical textual research.

Our intention in producing this book is to pass on some of our experience to a wider circle of readers in the Nordic countries and, not least, in the rest of the world.

1. On our way across the terrain of educational texts we begin with an article by **Nils Aage Jensen**, a historian who is an experienced author of textbooks. He tells about the many different "rooms" around educational texts: physical, linguistic, critical, economic and legal, to name but a few.

2. The next article is by the educational theorist **Karsten Schnack**. It presents the connections between educational theories and the actual

composition of textbooks, discussing in the process some fundamental questions concerning textbooks: are they, for example, to be **learnt** or to be **learnt from**?

3. The third article establishes the perspective of the reader. Here **Kirsten Haastrup**, researcher in foreign language teaching, discusses various views of reading and comprehension, and determines the desirable qualities of the good language-teaching text from the viewpoint of its receiver, the learner.

4. Next, **Egil Børre Johnsen**, an author and researcher of textbooks, deals with the relationship between fiction and faction in textbooks, giving contemporary international examples and citing his own experience. He is a spokesman for seeing textbooks as a form of literary art.

The two articles that follow discuss curricula as a special group of educational texts.

5. **Sten Sjørslev**, who is appointed in the Danish Ministry of Education, gives an inside report on the work at present in process on a curriculum reform for the whole of the Danish Folkeskole. This article gives insight into the forces which play a role in the creation of teaching guides today. And to conclude with, Sjørslev draws up criteria for an estimation of the curriculum as an eductional text.

6. In his article, the historian **Vagn Oluf Nielsen** conducts an analysis of the most recent curricula for history as a subject in the Folkeskole. He determines the status of the curriculum as historical source, and demonstrates the most important political mechanisms which can be associated with curricula as administratively directive instruments.

7. In the seventh article of *Text and Quality*, the focus is on the consequences which curricula have for textbooks. Here the physicists **Peter Norrild** and **Helene Sørensen** write about two contemporary materials for teaching their subject, and thereby indicate two very different options for the teachers, publishers and authors whose job it is to create cohesion between the various components – historical, exemplifying, factual and experimental – which coexist within the framework of modern scientific teaching material.

8. In continuation of this theme, the mathematician **Else Marie Pedersen** conducts an analysis of two modern mathematics books designed for the first year of the Gymnasium. The analysis concludes with a detailed characterisation of the good teaching text for mathematics in the 1990s.

9. In the next article the educationalist and philosopher **Sven Erik Nordenbo** determines the implications of the requirement that primary sources should be included in the teaching of philosophy in the Gymnasium, interpreting this requirement on the basis of the theory of science and value theory, and concluding with a specification of the consequences of these interpretations in the context of theories of education and curriculum theory.

10. The tenth article in the book turns to the question of how best to use photographs in foreign language teaching. **Marie-Alice Séférian**, researcher in foreign language teaching, analyses the interplay between text and picture in four French primers which are widely used internationally. On this basis Séférian formulates a number of conclusions concerning the appropriate selection and usage of photographs in foreign language teaching. The self-activation of the pupils is an important consideration in this context.

11. The next article deals with a new type of text whis has hardly received any notice as yet. Literary researcher **Susanne V. Knudsen** and media researcher **Birgitte Tufte** cite concrete examples in their account of using teenagers' **own** leisure activities as teaching texts. Hip hop and rap texts can capture the pupils' attention: but is it right to bring these leisure texts into the classroom? And if so, how should it be done?

12. Literary sociologist **Torben Weinreich** gives a statistical overview in his article of the modern educational textmarket. He sums up developments in the sales of textbooks over recent decades, and gives a number of explanations for these tendencies. To conclude, he offers a (provocative) formula for determining the quality of the modern textbook.

13. The general quality of textbooks is also a central preoccupation of **Kurt Hartvig Petersen's** article. Petersen, an expert on the school library system in Denmark, gives a brief account of the ongoing debate in this field and on the basis of his own experience provides a number of quality criteria which can be used when a selection is to be made from the enormous variety of books and other material available today.

14. In the fourteenth article the educationalist **Staffan Selander** takes stock of recent years' research in Sweden and internationally on "pedagogic" texts and their quality. To conclude with, Selander draws up some proposals for further research in the field of educational texts.

15.   With the fifteenth and final article **Peder Skyum-Nielsen**, rhetorician and leader of the research group behind this book, presents an overall model for understanding and describing the many circumstances which today are associated with 'educational texts'. Skyum-Nielsen's article summarises the descriptive method which the research group has developed to enable it to navigate successfully throughout the areas covered by *Text and Quality*.

The Rooms around Educational Texts

Nils Aage Jensen

What happens inside a book when it's closed? H. C. Andersen could have given us a good story about the games the letters play inside closed books. There they stand on the shelves with their backs to us. We think they're full of experiences and useful knowledge but we can't really be sure. Anything can be going on behind that silent binding. Not until the moment that we open the book do the letters find their places and form familiar words. The text does not exist until we start reading. A meeting is needed before communications are established.

The Norwegian author Agnar Mykle spent many years of his life writing just for himself. He requested that his piles of manuscript should be destroyed unread as soon as he was dead – the stupidest thing I've ever heard.

Perhaps it gave Mykle great satisfaction to think and write for himself alone, but such a solitary pleasure is completely trivial, not worth wasting words on. Sometimes I think that those pages were completely empty. Maybe he was simply pretending to be writing. Maybe he had nothing to say. Maybe every blessed evening he filed away a wad of blank sheets in his enormous archive and simply let the myth of his precious secrets blossom. And so what?

Writing does not become a reality until text meets reader. So the meeting-place is not without significance. Reading creates an inner room where the text unfurls, but it would be a big mistake to ignore the meaning of the outer room where the meeting takes place.

"The rooms around educational texts" is the title of this article, and it is to be taken quite literally. By a "room" is meant a place where the text spends time with its reader or author. Since an educational text has many aspects and facets, many levels and many effects, a great variety of rooms must be taken into account. I am now going to explore some of them.

The physical room

People read in many places. Some read sunk in their favourite arm-chair with a cup at their hand and sweet music in their ears. Many read in bed, though there are so many other things to do there. Some read on the train, where reading has a quite different function. Some read in tears at the dining table when they just can't learn their bloody maths. In little crowded apartments some sit on the toilet with a book so that they can have **peace** for a moment. Some read in the park stretched out on the grass all the long summer's day. Some people take texts to the chalet when they go skiing.

And let us not forget the hushed reading room in the library, or the teacher reading aloud to her class. There's reading going on everywhere.

The point is that the meeting of text and reader takes its colour from the physical room where it takes place. One does not get the same from a text which is read in noisy or degrading conditions as from the one that is read in inspiring and comfortable surroundings. Just cast your mind back. Think of texts you have read and learnt from and try to recall the scene. People who read a lot are apt to make much of their favourite reading place. Unconsciously we know quite well that one must be happy with one's surroundings if one is to have the full bene-fit of what one is reading. A whole theory of teaching reading has been developed from this one viewpoint: "You can learn the most amazing amount as long as you're comfortable and relaxed". This theory hasn't many legs to stand on but it has grasped something important: that the room affects the text. And this may be especially true of texts which have to be learnt, educational texts.

An analysis of educational texts will hardly be complete without a consideration of the physical conditions in which the text is used. Nor will it be quite without interest to know something of the physical con-ditions in which it was created. Examples are legion, from the poet in the garret to Luther at Wartburg, or for that matter Karl Marx in Soho.

The linguistic room

There are rooms for language. It is always in one of these that texts are created. Consider a text whose aim is to inform the staff of a business company about matters in their own and the firm's interests. Every company develops its own linguistic room, and this is reflected in the text. Texts pinned up on the privates' notice board in a barracks have a quite different tone to that used by a priest addressing his congregation in the parish magazine. This might appear self-evident, but if one begins to listen to texts from the point of view of their rooms the experience can be quite amazing. It is in their linguistic rooms that schools and other education institutions show characteristic traits. Enter beneath the eagle gazing into the light of heaven and you'll find yourself in a very different linguistic room from the one you were in a moment ago when you stood at the hot-dog van. The consequences are of course far-reaching when the moment comes to deal with educational texts, i.e. texts which communicate information. We are well aware of this and are working at it throughout society. We appoint communications experts – linguistic technicians – to solve the problems that arise when people move from one linguistic room to another. As Shaw demonstrated in Pygmalion, the relation between linguistic rooms is possibly one of the greatest social complications we have.

Of course it makes a difference who comes into the linguistic room. Roughly speaking, it may be the author or the reader. Huge amounts of work are being done on the reader's encounter with the text: reading proficiency, comprehension, everything that takes place on the receiver's side of the linguistic room. It's probably one of the most worked-on fields of all in textual research. In contrast, it is more rare for anyone to shed light on the author's side, but it can be interesting to analyse an educational text from the point of view of the author's linguistic approach to the work. Here is an example:

Most editors or reviewers will recognize three linguistic phases in the composition of an educational text. These won't be evident in the work of an experienced writer but will be clearly visible in that of a beginner. They can be characterized thus:

1. The language of the text displays some hesitancy and seems to be feeling its way forward. This results in uncertainty and a rather shaky sequence of sentences.

2. The language begins to flow more easily. The author is steady on her feet now, is clear about where she is heading and what regard must be paid to the reader.

3. The author is fascinated by her topic and is writing fluently. The

subject takes control of the writing and regard for the reader will often disappear in this phase.

It can sometimes be necessary to be aware of the phase the writing is in when one analyzes an educational text.

The reading room

The technical problems of reading have become something of a national cause. As mentioned above, this is probably the area where most research is done. We will leave that side of things in peace. However, in the reading room we again encounter some characteristic approaches to the text. Perhaps it is most appropriate to speak of certain psychological states connected with the reader's encounter with the written word. And here too we find three states, though they may seem a little awkward:

1. "I have to"-reading
2. "I want to"-reading
3. "I can't help it"-reading.

In this room an analysis of educational texts could deal with the extent to which they meet the special needs of a reader in one of these states.

With educational texts which function as part of an extensive learning process the first state will no doubt not be unfamiliar. Much of the content is seen as necessary but boring, and an effort of the will is needed to sit down and learn it. Reading for exams may serve as an example.

State no. 2 can be described as reading purely for pleasure, everything from the comics and Tarzan books of childhood to the greedy adult appetite for "the compact writings of Kant and Kierkegaard" (Halfdan Rasmussen). Obviously, anything can be read in this state, which only requires interest and commitment. Often the interesting point is whether the text simply satisfies a commitment that already exists or whether it is able to arouse interest in itself. One can speak of a commitment curve rising from zero to infinity. Where does this particular text intersect with the curve, and why?

A little investigation that I conducted in Nyborg State Prison on the reading habits of the inmates gives a very clear picture of the extremes. For some, their favourite reading was exciting and dramatic but above all escapist. It might be thrillers or porn magazines, or, if non-fiction, books on occult subjects like UFOs or ghosts, the motto being "anywhere: out of the world!" By contrast, another group was much more absorbed in the close reading of laws and statutes that had to do with their particular situation, everything from the regulation of justice to social security. In other words, they were reading educational texts which were especially close to their reality. The immediate question was whether in this latter group the texts were congruent with the "state".

Perhaps state no. 3 is somewhat overlooked, probably because it seems so self-evident. But this is where the most interesting perspectives may appear. This state comprises texts that are highly educational, texts whose content it is imperative to communicate even to the reluctant reader. These days a sign saying "No ads please!" is found on many Danish mailboxes. This is a signal from the owner that she is fed up of reading the huge quantities of brightly coloured junk mail that are delivered every day, and has decided to put a stop to it by affixing the aforesaid sign. But it isn't possible to protect oneself from "educational texts" when out on the street. They hit you in the eye from windows, walls and street signs. It can be fatal to ignore some of them (max. 30 km), whilst others are felt to be irritatingly importunate. Some you need to read, others annoy you, but in both cases they are texts which you cannot help reading. It is not by chance that the cartons of breakfast cereals are sprinkled with educational text. The reader is in a perfect situation, sitting defenselessly in front of the text, prevented from screaming her disgust (or enthusiasm) across the room by the food in her mouth.

How far texts like this affect us, or what interplay there is between the design of the texts and the reader, the advertisers will be able to tell. But as far as I know, no studies have been made of such involuntary reading that regards the texts as educational phenomena. So here is another area which can be profitably included in the analysis of educational texts.

The judgement room

Whether an educational text is **good** or **bad** is naturally dependent on the criteria used to judge it. In the judgement rooms sit not only professional analysts and reviewers but also users, both educators and the students and pupils who are the primary recipients. Each group has a number of criteria, many of which will be common to all of them though with a different order of priority. Briefly and banally, it can be claimed that a **good** educational text is one that everyone concerned agrees is good. It has to satisfy everyone's favourite evaluative basis.

There have been numerous attempts to draw up a list of evaluative criteria in order of importance, but closer investigation reveals that such a list cannot be universally valid because it must necessarily focus on the needs of only one of the interested parties.

It is fundamentally difficult to imagine a disinterested analysis of an educational text. It can also be hard to see the point of such an analysis. In most cases, an analysis is simply synonymous with an evaluation. This has been constantly demonstrated in the work carried out by the research group behind *Text and Quality*. We can't disassemble the machine without commenting approvingly or critically on the separate parts or on how they "ought" to have been put together.

We expect a review to offer an evaluation which can serve to convince us that we should or should not take the trouble to read a certain book. With educational texts, the reviewer's judgement will often result in a decision to buy or not buy the book or material. When there is confusion in the judgement room the losers are usually the ones who have most difficulty making themselves heard or who have the least precise criteria. These will often be the pupils, who are the primary consumers. But in the last resort they are probably the ones who are most competent, on their own criteria, to judge the book, and this is problematic. In all events it's terribly noisy in the evaluators' room: authors bawling out reviewers, teachers bawling out authors and reviewers, and their accusations being countered. The voice of the pupil is the only one not heard. In 1992 the Norwegian association of non-fiction writers tried to rectify this situation to some extent when they drew up "the reviewer's Ten Commandments", with the intention of training reviewers to pay the necessary regard to the criteria of other groups.

An analysis of educational texts in the judgement room ought perhaps to focus on the mutual relevance of criteria.

NFF-NYTT 6/1992.

The media room

This article has not made a sharp distinction between text and pictures. But it is not possible to discuss the rooms around an educational text without also glancing into the room where media differentiation takes place. This is a historical room, with a retrospective exhibition of the media which have hitherto transmitted the educational text. Starting from the Dead Sea Scrolls or the rune stones we stroll past the Book of Kells and other wonderful things, then past palaeotypes and incunabulae to the age of the xylograph. A short step brings us to the photographic plate, after which everything speeds up and ends in a chaos of possibilities. Enter electronics and digitalization. The production of texts increases explosively, but so does the production of programmes to keep control of it all. The possibilities of merging texts, searching for information and processing illustrations have been multiplied, and today we have more options than anyone can really grasp.

Oddly enough, our eyes are usually firmly fixed on future possibilities whilst what is behind us sinks into oblivion. This is close to a catastrophe when a text is analyzed, since every text is dependent on the medium that transmits it. This is not only important in the phase of creation but also when the text is communicated and received. The controversy surrounding the publication of the Dead Sea Scrolls can serve as an extreme example. They cannot be generally read until they are transferred to another medium, so a jump has to be made from the oldest form of transmission to the most up-to-date. And so many interests are involved – religious, linguistic, economic and many others – that the whole project goes to ground.

Coming closer to home, the problems surrounding the media situation will also affect texts and their uses. A generation ago it was normal for school books to use a variety of typographies simply because it was felt to be necessary for future readers to know that there were several sorts of alphabets, in this case the Latin and the Gothic. Obviously the content of the text was coloured by the typography it was printed in. Every software firm is extremely conscious of this.

In Denmark there is a famous Latin textbook by Kristian Mikkelsen; but I doubt whether its renowned first sentence, "Italia terra est", would have made such an impact if the book had been printed in "curly letters". In our first encounter with a type of text the typography has special importance in determining our subsequent view of the content. This will be far more significant in our computerized age as the printing and viewing options are enormously more varied than previously.

An analysis of educational texts cannot avoid including the transmission options – the choice of medium.

The legal/economic room

One is seriously mistaken if one imagines that educational texts should be independent of the legal circumstances of their creation. The law actually has an enormous influence on their form and range. Let us examine a few examples.

Suppose an author to have strolled through the aforesaid rooms taking all reasonable care. His idea, his educational and didactic considerations, are all viable, and the methodology is fully worked out. Now for the writing, the organization, the layout ... Then come discussions of the illustrations, the sound-tape, the media form, the follow-ups, and anything else relevant. But now reality invades the dream world: we can't use that picture because someone owns the copyright and won't release it. That quotation can't stand: it's prohibited. This information is covered by intellectual property rights and can't be cited before the owner has published it himself. The printers are on strike, and in the meantime your main character dies and his archives are tied up. The possibilities for creating the optimal text which the author has dreamt of are reduced time and time again by such irritations as these. But the influence of the law does not end here. Later on the budget has to be thought of. What is the cost of the pictures necessary to make the text authoritative? How can the budget be balanced to ensure publication? Which scholarly journal will take the article and under which economic circumstances? Will the text end up in a database, and what will that mean for the finished product? Et cetera.

The possibilities for intrusive influence on the text are numerous in the legal room, usually far more than the author has been able to imagine. The length of the book and extent of its content are extremely weighty factors in planning the text: financial considerations invariably force the author to cut his text. It should be emphasized that very few texts come into the world in the form they were originally conceived. In our day it is rarely possible for authors to ignore external factors such as copyright law (for quotations), public lending rights (when thinking about the financial aspect), organizational agreements and publishing contracts (am I allowed to write this?) etc., etc., etc.

A work of non-fiction is often prefaced with a list of acknowledgements giving credit and thanks to everyone concerned, up to the author's mother-in-law and cat. One might wish that all this gratitude was followed by a list of circumstances which **prevented** the text from appearing in the form it was intended. Acknowledgements of ingratitude. If the promoter and primary user had such a list available it would be more possible to evaluate and analyze the text. But this no doubt is a cultural impossibility.

These comments might invite one to reflect on what a text could have been if its originator had been allowed his head. If one compares this with the future possibilities of computerized word processing such an "analysis of the absent" may not be quite in vain.

Other rooms?

There are many apartments in the house where the educational text develops. One could move on to **the social room**, where political conditions influence the text. Many dreary texts have come into being because the publishers (never, of course, the author) did not dare issue the book or material as it stood and so requested yet another rewriting. The shape of the text can be determined by moral or religious considerations. This may be due to the inner censor which most people submit to when they write, often without realizing it. But obviously the opposite is also just as common: the author may appear coarser than she really is, because even provocation can be part of the educational technique. All non-fiction writing, and thus all educational texts, are in reality contributions to debate. Either they can try to gain the readers' support by soft-pedalling "dangerous" messages or they can invite debate.

One room in the house is so large that it almost has space for all the others. We can call it **the artistic room**. Unfortunately it may often appear rather bare. Possibly – and hopefully – the future will show that this room is one of the most important of all in the formation of educational texts. For as the Norwegian textbook writer Egil Børre Johnsen put it: "[...] there's something called textbook art. We just haven't found it properly yet."

I think we have to look for it in the house with many rooms.

Educational Texts in the Light of General Didactics

Karsten Schnack

People have always educated their children, and since the rise of writing, and especially after the development of printing, texts have played a central role in this process. We have only a limited knowledge of the function of texts in "everyday" teaching through the ages; but as schools developed into separate, independent institutions, special types of texts emerged to serve as teaching materials.

These texts have been among the most widely read of all, and many textbooks have been something of a cultural institution right up to our own times. In the refrain of a nonsense song in a popular Advent calendar for 1991 there are the words "I can hop. I can run. It is very, very fun". Inquiry among my acquaintance has shown that even the youngsters know that this is a reference to "the book the old people learnt English from". It is actually the opening of a primer in English published by the famous linguist Otto Jespersen (1895), in which he introduced both phonetic script and pictures to pave the way for short conversations in English.

It is scarcely possible to speak about school textbooks in general terms; the different subjects and areas have very different problems and traditions. The texts and their quality must be seen in relation to such matters as subject, culture, tradition, expectations, norms in the population, the assumptions of pupils and teachers etc. They are also related to theories of teaching and basic educational ideas.[1] I will give an account of these matters below before considering a number of contemporary dilemmas.

The relation to theories of teaching

The following will relate some classical examples of teaching theories which illustrate the correlation between teaching form and what is required from particular types of teaching material.

1.

Retskrivning.

I can hop. I can run.
See me hop! See me run!
It is fun, fun, fun!

I can hop on one leg.
Can you? Yes. Let me
see if you can. Yes, that
is very good.

Udtale.

ai kän håp. ai kän rʌn.
si· mi· håp! si· mi· rʌn!
it iz fʌn, fʌn, fʌn.

ai kän håp ån wʌn leg. kän ju·? jes. — let mi· si·
if ju· kän. jes, ðät iz veri gud.

O. Jespersen and C. Sarauw: Engelsk Begynderbog. ("English primer"). Copenhagen 1895.

In practice there is of course a correlation: the nature of the material arises largely from a certain idea about the nature of teaching, whilst the form of the material will naturally influence and maintain conceptions of teaching.

Throughout time, progressive teachers wishing to demolish the established paradigm have in the midst of their attempts to conquer the school's general suppressive tendencies had the frustrating experience of being asked by the pupils (and their parents) whether they were not going to be taught something soon. This usually means that they expect to start using textbooks.

There is nothing surprising in this. Psychologically, it has to do with feelings of security, and sociologically with power and opportunities for upward mobility. If textbooks reflect or illustrate the curriculum in force at any given time, it is not strange that they are regarded as a power factor which one will be penalized for ignoring. At best, it will be a waste of time. For this reason alternative teaching and textbooks are also regarded as dangerous; in many countries there is a long tradition that they must have official approval.

The Bell and Lancaster method, known as Mutual Teaching, which enjoyed a measure of popularity in the first half of the 19th century, is a classical illustration of the relationship between theory and material. One teacher was in charge of a large number of pupils who were placed in smaller groups with each an elder pupil as monitor. Work proceeded with military discipline, the "textbooks" being lessons written out on boards which were read aloud by the pupils in chorus when the teacher gave the signal. In the Danish system there were 80 boards to teach reading, 100 for writing, 120 for maths and fifteen for geography.

A second example which is perhaps just as significant is the long tradition of catechizing. Luther's Catechism, with the Explanation of Pontoppidan and later the Textbook of Bishop Balle, were the dominant schoolbooks for generations of Danish children. Lessons proceeded like a kind of examination, with the books composed in the form of brief questions and answers which the pupils had to learn by heart. The tradition for this model goes back to one of the greatest successes in the history of the textbook, *De Partibus*, a Latin primer written by Ælius Donatus in 350 AD, which was the quintessential textbook for many centuries. Luther knew his Donatus. All this was in the days before there were sufficient books and the central elements of education were learning by heart and examination by the teacher.

For most people today, traditional classroom teaching is probably closely associated with textbooks. Lessons are often in two parts: first revision of the last lesson and then continuation to the next stage. Pupils were never meant to be able to read their textbooks on their own without help from their teachers.

An interesting genre connected with this form of teaching was developed at the beginning of the 19th century, first in Germany (F.E. Rochow) and later in Denmark. This was the Reading Book for schools, a kind of compendium of everything worth knowing, like the adults' encyclopedias.

With increasing division into subjects 'Danish' took over the more general material. However, textbooks for the subject Danish eventually developed into collections of literary texts, and thus specialized text-books originated.

The last example that will be mentioned here is "individualized teaching", which gained a certain following in Denmark in the 30s and gave rise to experimentation. Washburne's *Adjusting the School to the Child*, 1932, was translated in 1937. The material for beginners made a great impression, and inspired such projects as "Individualized Number Training" 1939 ff. in Denmark and the other Nordic countries.

Individualized teaching makes special demands on the books used. The material must be: 1. graduated, 2. suitable for self-instruction and 3. with automatical assessment. Exercises and puzzle-solving have become the dominant activities.

The relation to basic educational ideas

In my introduction I claimed that people have always educated their children. In principle there have been two different approaches: knowledge can be simply transmitted by getting the pupils to remember and imitate; or the pupils can be encouraged to take a stand on what they are taught and how they are taught it, and to work independently.

Historically, transmission has been the most important job of schools and indeed the whole education system. At the start of the 19th century Humboldt's new University in Berlin inaugurated a break with this tradition, based on the idea of general personal education (Bildung). For the first time the main task of the students was not to write down exactly what the teacher said in order to be able repeat it later as precisely as possible. Now they were supposed to immerse themselves in the subject, with the aim of personal development. And the university was required to be not simply a teaching institution but also a research centre.

But in aristocratic fashion these ideas only applied to a tiny part of the adult population. And like most other authorities, Humboldt clearly thought that children and young people still had to be guided by their teachers, to cram and to repeat their lessons, just as in the catechizing method described above.

Throughout our century, the general processes of democratization have gone hand in hand with another view of child-rearing, largely inspired by psychoanalysis, to turn these ideas upside down to some extent. Ideas of personal development have often fared better in primary schools, with more and more emphasis being placed on ready knowledge and correct learning as the children get older.

Even today these two views are still opposed to each other, with various conceptions of what useful knowledge consists of. The basic question which this situation gives rise to is whether textbooks are to be regarded as materials to **learn** or to **learn from**.

Dilemmas

1. The responsibilities of subject didactics

There is a fundamental question of didactic responsibility connected with the discussion of textbooks. Who decides what the pupils ought to be taught, the order in which they are taught it and the methods to be used? There are national and local curricula, but these are formulated in such general terms that they are wide open to interpretation and varieties of implementation. And many teachers do not seem particularly interested in referring to these texts in the normal run of things.

From one point of view it would seem to be the job of the subject didactics experts to fill out the broad outlines of the curriculum. It amounts to a subject in itself to work with subject didactic questions. Those who possess the special expertise which it requires can utilize their insight in textbooks or textbook systems which may to some extent be authorized and which can be said to constitute the curriculum in practice.

From another point of view, it is an integral part of a teacher's professionalism to be able to assume responsibility for the didactics of his or her subject and thus to be able to relate to the textbooks quite freely. This is the official attitude in Denmark, one of the reasons being that otherwise the statutory provision for the participation of parents and pupils in decision-making will be without any real foundation.

The first viewpoint is not without advantages. It ensures a systematic progression of work, and at its best can guard against too much arbitrariness and hobbyhorsery. On the other hand it can easily result in a textbook tyranny which limits the opportunities for adapting the teaching to the interests of the pupils and to the conditions and events of the day. With textbook systems especially (in such subjects as mathematics and languages) the curricular options can easily be limited to the first choice made among various systems, if indeed the school's economy allows such a choice.

2. Educationalized texts

In extension of the above, there is a dilemma concerning the tendency of textbook authors to incorporate their ideas about teaching in their books. There is clearly a need for plenty of clear and simple writing on all sorts of subjects. Schools need popularized texts, in the best sense of the term. But it is to be questioned whether schools benefit from what may be called "educationalized texts".

The problem is somewhat ironic, because it is often progressive authors with many good ideas for activating the pupils and with an interest in alternative learning processes who produce books which **represent** exciting teaching but do not necessarily stimulate it.

Educationalized material may be constructed with a logic which reflects a progressive course of teaching based on the pupils' anticipated realizations and questions. Read as a kind of report on a completed teaching project, or as a teacher's plan of a specific course, it can be very convincing; but as teaching material its effect can be quite different from that intended, as the pupils are guided through the subject by questions which they themselves have not asked. It is not **their** curiosity which governs the proceedings.

Another type of educationalized material is often quite informally organized around topics but is characterized by the author's numerous suggestions for discussion, exercises, activities, and investigations. Many of these suggestions are not very promising and thus deserve criticism, but this is not actually a problem or dilemma. My real point here is that even when the exercises, experiments and other activities are reasonable enough there is a problem of principle in that they are part of the total text of the book, even though they may be printed in separate boxes or some such device.

A lesson may have been good because there was the imagination and energy to perform such activities, but the same success will not automatically result if other pupils in other classes perform the same activities simply because they are in the book. Educationally there is a great difference between what we may call "school experiments" and what it means to investigate the world experimentally. There is, moreover, a great difference between solving problems set by others and discussing which problems it would be interesting to solve.

The authors and publishers who have stakes in educationalized material do not necessarily disagree with this problematization. The view is often advanced that strong teachers with plenty of energy and initiative can simply use the books as they choose, whilst the exercises are intended primarily as a help for their weaker colleagues whose teaching might otherwise be rather traditional and boring.

This is undeniably a point. However, the important question is whether this kind of help is not often a disservice, making the less resourceful teacher appear even weaker and less involved with the subject by reducing him or her to a mere administrator of an educationalized textbook.

A number of surveys confirm the general impression that textbooks are rarely used in the way the authors intended. A separate teachers' book will not become dog-eared. However, this might stimulate the authors to educationalize the book still further: if all the good suggestions are inserted in the text itself there might be a greater likelihood of their being used. But according to Swedish investigations (JOHANSSON 1988), teachers are guided in their practice more by the content and thematics of the book than by methodical instructions and ideas.

Many of the thoughts and ideas incorporated into educationalized material ought perhaps to be transferred to the texts discussed during the in-service training and further professional qualification of teachers. But the publishing houses do not normally show much interest in texts with such a purpose.

3. The style of textbooks

Even though textbooks are of many different types, the normal impression is that stylistically they are typically distinct from other kinds of writing. It is surprising to encounter one that isn't. Their great variety makes it difficult to define this stylistic uniformity, but one characteristic which suggests itself is their particular jargon, which appears to have survived despite much criticism and ridicule. Here I am thinking of such classical formulations as: "It is clear from this", or "as is clearly shown above", or "as you might suppose".

But the tendency to use a more limited form of language than other discursive writing may be more crucial. This can be explained in two ways: firstly, the authors wish to produce texts which can be easily understood by readers of limited experience and competence; and secondly, they wish to create or maintain a form of objectivity by using the familiar style of short articles in handbooks.

This is a genuine problem. Each of these endeavours is respectable, but it is still regrettable that explanations become more one-sided and texts occasionally almost incomprehensible in their attempts to deal briefly and simply with matters that are abstract and complicated. What is perhaps particularly interesting here is the obvious tendency of textbooks to tone down what an investigation by Avon Crismore (CRISMORE 1984) calls "metadiscourse", i.e. the author's often stylistically implicit "discoursing about the discourse".

This tendency can make the books duller, but the main problem is that it gives them the appearance of being objective, incontrovertible sources of information which prevents them from being related to as texts. It might be a premise for a better and more critical use of textbooks that they are treated as texts whilst they are being used, and are subjected to some of the analytical tools which the pupils are taught to use on other kinds of texts.

4. The power of example

In all communicative exercises, in popularization and even in basic scientific research a fine balance has to be maintained between the concrete and the abstract. The concrete often has the effect of seeming alive, real and graspable. The subject will become more generalized and theoretical as more of its aspects are turned into abstractions when they are not relevant in the given context. General knowledge is based on abstract and theoretical concepts and relations, but concrete exemplifications are often needed if one is to envisage, understand and absorb the content as more than rote learning.

Good examples are worth gold in the educational process. They are eloquent and memorable. But does the learner also remember what they are examples of? Examples have great power. One cannot imagine teaching, or perhaps even textbooks, without concrete examples. But the more they appeal to identification and motivation the greater the risk that they will also keep the idea on the concrete level and inhibit a deeper understanding of the general principle which the example was intended to illustrate.

On the basis of developmental psychology it can be argued that this dilemma will be the greater in proportion to the youth of the intended users of the textbook; but its core is never outgrown.

A variety of examples of "the same thing" can of course be of great help, but one must always realize that theoretical concepts and the relations between them are not empirical generalizations, and one should not give one's pupils the impression that they are, in one's eagerness to relate what is abstract to something concrete.

5. Overloaded textbooks

The ancient Romans used to say that stuffing a pupil with learning is like pouring wine into a carafe: if the opening is wide one can pour vigorously, but if it is narrow more caution is needed. Less wine will get in through the narrow opening in the same space of time, but it will still be a greater quantity than if it was poured rapidly, as in that case it would only have splashed about everywhere and none would have ended up in the carafe.

This image suffers from its conception of the pupil as passive, with the implicit metaphor of the "tabula rasa", but none the less the reminder of the necessity of differentiation is valuable. Overloaded textbooks which are **too** difficult do not teach anything. Or worse: they can result in paralysis and mystification.

But the problem is that rules cannot be made for how fast the wine should be poured. A text can scarcely be judged to be too easy or too difficult unless it is seen in relation to the specific purpose for which it is intended.

6. The problem of the good textbook

A textbook is made to be used and should be judged by its utility. What opportunities does it present in the educational context of which it is a part? Analyses of textbooks which overlook this perspective have little value for the teacher.

But it can be difficult to maintain this perspective. To start with, teaching is very varied and can be seen in so many ways. Furthermore, analysts may often state that they have such an aim in view and yet embark on comprehensive objective analyses of books quite detached from their (possible) use. And there are certain paradoxes and dilemmas involved in this problem which overall could be formulated as "the problem of the good textbook".

Mediocre material draws out the good teacher, or at least permits his or her personality to emerge. The material as text will almost certainly provoke a response. Furthermore, the teacher – both as a person and as a professional – will probably appear more exciting in the context of a book which is no fun or even downright bad.

On the other hand, the "good textbook" can easily come to dominate lesson time which ought to be governed by the teacher and the pupils. It can even make a whole discipline stagnate, as ironically enough was the case in the training of teachers in Denmark in the years following 1966, when a new course designed to qualify future teachers to plan their own teaching independently was completely paralysed by a "good textbook". Furthermore, as G.R. Rabe wrote in *Pedagogisk tidskrift* ("Educational Journal") in 1865, "an almost perfect textbook has no doubt often had an inhibitive effect on the teacher's own development" (JOHANSSON 1988 p. 7).

Conclusion

The last quotation demonstrates that textbooks and their function have long been problematized. This is completely necessary. But it is not realistic to envisage a whole school system without textbooks. This would be an absurd ideal in our modern textualized society. The electronic revolution does not change matters fundamentally, though it certainly makes it plain that our relation to the text has changed.

It is understandable that the Vikings had a somewhat solemn attitude to the primitive texts which they laboriously engraved on boulders, but today it would be absurd to attribute so much significance to a text.

Mention is often made of the educational triangle, consisting of the teacher, the pupil and the subject. Previously it has often been the case that the textbook has comprised the subject. Today it ought to be clear that the textbook, whether printed or electronic, is only one medium in the educational process.

The "subject" is a matter for continual cultural and democratic debate, a process which is undoubtedly seen as constantly threatened. In the Nordic countries this finds expression nowadays in anxieties about the national cultural identity which are connected with both widespread decentralization and incorporation in the larger international communities. Warnings are also issued against tendencies to cultural disintegration and the difficult conditions for democratic debate if society is not founded on a communal frame of reference. Proponents of this view have gone so far as to say that the content of this frame of reference is less important than the fact of its being communal.

In such a situation it is hardly surprising to encounter the idea that it is the job of the schools to unite the people. Thus there is a renewed interest in various forms of curricular canons – and this includes textbooks. But to use textbooks to protect us against experienced tendencies towards cultural disintegration is a reactionary misunderstanding.

"Textbooks are curriculum in practice" is a slogan which is more and more often quoted. In recent years there has been a trend to turn investigations of textbooks (and their official sanctioning, in countries where such practices exist) into an exact science, as if education was a case of the pupils learning what is in the books. But in a modern society pupils must learn to deal with texts in a way which is both more relaxed and more critical. They must also learn to handle and classify previously unimaginable quantities of information. Teaching materials are and will remain only some of the media they learn from.

But textbooks are of interest in many ways. It is still the common view that good teaching material is the precondition for good teaching. And many interest groups and organizations, both public and private, have a heavy stake in teaching material. It is regarded as the path to influence, a stage in the struggle for a generation's consciousness. Pupils must learn to reflect on that.

Note

1. In this article 'didactics' is used as a translation of the German and Scandinavian concept 'Didaktik', which means something like "curriculum studies and educational theory".

Bibliography

APPLE, M.W. & L.K. CHRISTIAN-SMITH (eds.): *The Politics of the Textbook*. London, Routledge 1991.

BJØRNDAL, B.: *Et studium i lærebøkenes didaktikk.* ("A study in the didactics of the textbook"). Oslo, Pedagogisk forskningsinstitutt 1982.

CRISMORE, A.: The Rhetoric of Textbooks: Metadiscourse. In: *Journal of Curriculum Studies 16:3*, 1984.

JESPERSEN, O. & SARAUW, C.: *Engelsk Begynderbog.* ("English primer"). Copenhagen, Det Schubotheske Forlag 1895.

JOHANSSON, M.: Den omöjliga läroboken. ("The impossible textbook"). In: *Skolböcker 3*. Stockholm, Utbildningsdepartementet 1988.

JOHNSEN, E.B.: *Textbooks in the Kaleidoscope. A Critical Survey of Literature and Research on Educational Texts*. Oslo, Scandinavian University Press 1993.

SKOVGAARD-PETERSEN, V. et al.: *Skolebøger i 200 år.* ("Schoolbooks through 200 years"). Copenhagen, Gyldendal 1970.

Receivers' Perspective

Kirsten Haastrup

Up to now text quality has mainly been seen as a product of the author's or sender's efforts. In this article focus will be on the receiver or reader, and text quality will be discussed in relation to what he or she gets out of the reading. In relation to the model presented (on page 172 ff.) below, the present argument bears on areas 3, 4, 11 and 13.

Sender and receiver perspectives are complementary and thus of equal importance. The fact that the receiver's perspective is stressed in the following may give the impression that the sender viewpoint has been forgotten or is regarded critically. The purpose, however, is simply to warn against the often unfortunate outcome of emphasising the development from "sender's intention" to "completed text" at the expense of the later phase in the communication process, in which the reader grapples with the text. Text quality is a measure of the extent to which sender (author) and receiver (reader) understand one another, so reaching understanding should be regarded as a joint venture. Assuming that "student understanding" is the hallmark of a good educational text, it can indeed be claimed that for educational texts the receiver's perspective is not only important, it is crucial.

Throughout this article the argumentation will be based on situations in which the student or pupil is a reader of primary educational texts, typically textbooks.

From text adaptation to reader processing

The sender-viewpoint has been too prominent, I shall argue, in that educational texts have been analyzed almost exclusively as author products. Focus has been on the completed texts that are put before the pupil, and little or no attention has been paid to the way in which the reader has processed and understood the text. To underpin the claim we can cite the fact that researchers and teachers have traditionally been

Photo: Kirstine Theilgaard.

very concerned with measuring text readability. Quantitative measures such as readability formulae have been popular, as have more subjective assessments of readability, referred to as "verbal accessibility" or simply as the ease/difficulty of a text. A case in point is a recent Danish official report on the quality of teaching materials in schools (Ministry of Education 1994). The authors put forward their subjective assessment of the difficulty levels of a number of texts, quoting examples and criticizing specific text features which might impede reading, such as too long lines, no division lines between syllables (for beginners), and spelling variation. Another obvious example of text-texture focus comes from foreign language teaching, where authentic texts have been simplified and turned into "Easy readers" or adapted readers, mainly by means of abridgement and vocabulary control.

In these examples, then, readability is regarded as a feature of the text, and nothing is discovered about the processes through which the reader takes meaning from the text, i.e. arrives at an understanding of it.

What may be needed is a shift of focus from the text to the reader, more precisely from text adaptation to reader processing, or from text accessibility to pupil's independent text processing.

Let us now change the perspective to the situation where teachers assess or check their pupils' understanding of a given educational text. For a "traditional" lesson in, for example, history, the pupils' set homework has been five pages of a textbook. Part of the lesson is taken up with a teacher-led discussion on the basis of which the teacher tries to assess what the pupils as a group, or even as individuals, have got out of their reading. In countries other than Denmark this teacher-class dialogue may well be replaced by written multiple-choice questions or workbook exercises checking understanding.

In my view it is a shortcoming that we examine the pupils' understanding of a text as a product rather than take an interest in the process through which understanding is achieved. I wish to contend that in order to improve text quality, especially in educational texts, a process view must be adopted. We cannot discuss text readability without consulting the reader, and the reader's perspective is especially important in connection with textbooks.

For these reasons, a main line of argument throughout this article will be a plea for process focus. It might be objected that this is changing the subject and moving from a discussion of "how to get better texts" to "how to get better text users, i.e. readers"? My answer to this is that both issues are being discussed and that it is advantageous to merge them.

The psycholinguistic view: reading as an interactive process

Presupposing that literacy is a social construct, that there is little consensus about what is required to obtain meaning from a text, and that many perspectives are needed to paint a full picture, I shall restrict my discussion to the **psycholinguistic** perspective. This means omitting such important considerations as the affective domain and the aesthetics of reading. The following will not deal with the study of fiction, textual analysis or text interpretation. Imagine instead a pupil reading a textbook with the primary purpose of retrieving information. However, although we focus on the pupil's cognition, on her comprehension as understood by psycholinguistics, she may still, hopefully, have fun reading the book.

The interaction between linguistic and conceptual knowledge

Within the psycholinguistic interactive paradigm two different meanings of the term "interaction" are acknowledged. In one sense there is interaction of skills, meaning that the reader has, for example, syntactic and lexical skills which she brings to bear on the reading task. In another sense there is interaction between the reader and the text: in broad terms, each individual reader has her own reading of the text. The latter sense is close to the area which in literary studies is known as Reader-Response criticism.

The short exchange below is taken from Louise Erdrich's novel: *Love medicine* (ERDRICH 1984 p. 91). A young American-Indian boy studies "Moby Dick" at school, and back at the reservation his mother starts off the dialogue saying:

"You are always reading that book. What's in it?"
"The story of the great white whale".
She couldn't believe it. After a while she said:
"What do they got to wail about those whites?"

More than a simple mishearing is at work here. Firstly, linguistic knowledge and skills: the levels of phonology and orthography are activated. The words "whale" and "wail" are homonyms, both pronounced /weɪl/. What is decisive, however, is the mother's schemata about the whites. Since they are the privileged classes, and her oppressors, she cannot associate them with complaining and "wailing". In technical terms, she cannot reconcile what she hears (data information) with what she knows (conceptual knowledge stored as schemata). Both types of knowledge contribute to her "hearing" or comprehension.

The above point needs emphasizing, since we often see that readers' conceptual knowledge and linguistic skills are treated as two separate phenomena. Colleagues in the field of evaluating text books often have one chapter of their report in which they address such questions as: "What is the text's verbal accessibility?" The answer is given in terms of its score on a readability scale. Then there will be another chapter discussing whether the concepts introduced and the general level of abstraction in the text makes it suitable for the age group for which it is intended (Ministry of Education 1994). However, when, for instance, pupils read a geography text book, both their conceptual and linguistic skills are brought to bear and, optimally, work hand in hand during the reading process.

In the following section we shall look at different approaches to the study of "understanding", giving examples of relevant methods for studying comprehension processes. The first method highlights the connection between a reader's understanding of a text and her reasons for studying it.

A link between 'understanding' and 'doing'

In order to discover what the critical components of reading ability are, many researchers apply a method by which they study the reader's ability to give an oral or written summary of the text. They find that this offers a good measure of his or her understanding of the text. Part of the rationale for this is expressed by Grabe in the following way:

Fluent readers not only seek to comprehend a text when they read, they also evaluate the text information and compare/synthesize it with other sources of information/knowledge. Thus *synthesis and evaluation skills and strategies* are critical components of reading abilities. (GRABE 1991 p. 381)

The principal point of the argumentation is that the higher-order skills of synthesis and evaluation are crucial both for good reading and good summarizing. The quality of the summary thus reflects the informant's reading process.

In this connection speech act theory has a pivotal function. If the informant can recognize the rhetorical schemata of a text and identify such individual speech acts as illustrating, exemplifying, concluding etc. she has the prerequisite for making a good summary of it.

I will now refer briefly to two empirical studies that throw light on comprehension processes.

Brown and Day start from the assumption that "The ability to summarize information is an important study skill involving both comprehension of, and attention to, importance at the expense of trivia" (1983 p. 1). In a series of studies they analyze the way in which "experts" (college rhetoric teachers) and non-experts (freshman college students) write summaries of expository texts. Some of the main differences between the two groups were that the "experts" combined information from different parts of the text and had no problem in boiling down the main content to a 4-5-line sentence. In other words, they were able to formulate their own "topic sentence". In contrast the "non-experts" could not reformulate the main essence, but could only select one of the sentences from the text as the best candidate for the "topic sentence".

Thus the use of macrorules for summarizing seems to be a difficult and late developing skill.

A second example comes from CUMMING et al. (1989), who studied the thinking processes of adults when performing challenging reading and summarizing tasks. In one part of their study they focus on the problem-solving strategies used by undergraduates (native speakers of English) working with the English version of a piece of political journalism written by Lenin himself.

It is generally assumed that in order to perform a summary task, people construct a mental model of the significance of the text integrating first and foremost situational and propositional information. Cumming et al. tested this assumption by having their informants think aloud while reading. The extracts below are from the recorded and later transcribed think-aloud protocols about Bolsheviks at the beginning of this century.

> "Okay, so this guy, Plekhanov, has said in the newspaper, the Tovarishch, the Mensheviks, um, the Mensheviks want to have a "joint platform with the Cadets". But the Mensheviks themselves disagree with that in the Volkszeitung, which is unknown for the Russians and the Nasha Tribuna". (CUMMING et al. 1989 p. 209)

In the above text we have someone who starts out from a text quotation ("joint platform with the Cadets") and fits it into a larger situational representation.

A second informant, who is an even more successful reader/summarizer applies his own background knowledge in order to conceptualize the situational context of the passage.

> "This is very interesting, this part on the, um, the Mensheviks and the Duma, and supporting the Duma no matter what, and working within the system, because it reminds me that in the pre-World War One period, uh, among the uh, Bolsheviks there was a split over the problem of whether to work through the party system or whether not to [...]." (Ibidem p. 211)

Cumming et al. describe the informant's expertise thus:

> Fitting the passage into larger historical schemata, he was able to make informed interpretations based on background knowledge of the period in which the passage was originally written. (Ibidem)

This discussion of what informants can and cannot do with a text may have shifted our focus slightly. However, reader quality and text quality are closely related, and it would be interesting to see empirical studies which use expert readers as informants, and where one important criterion of a high-quality expository text is that it lends itself to or even elicits good summaries.

Reading as inferencing

Beyond the skills discussed above, readers' inferential skills are critical. Good reading depends on the ability to infer meaning. Readers' inferencing may include one or more of the following types of process: providing missing links in the text, making non-automatic connections, and filling in gaps or discontinuities in interpretation. Broadly defined, inferences are the connections people make when attempting to reach an interpretation of what they read or hear. (BROWN & YULE 1983).

With a view to the assessment of quality in textbooks, studies of readers' inferential processes would be highly useful. For instance, a study could be envisaged where readers think aloud as they read part of a chapter in a history textbook on the Danish resistance movement during the Second World War. The author of the book has the intention of being objective in the way he depicts such matters as the motives of the Danish saboteurs and the importance of sabotage activities for the liberation of Denmark from the German occupation. But what impression does the reader get? – not any reader, but one of the pupils for which the book is intended. Comprehension questions may be inserted in the various sections of the text in order to discover how the reader's understanding of and attitudes to the sabotage activities are gradually shaped. Only a careful recording of readers' comprehension processes can tell us what features of the text influence the reader, and how they do so.

Instead of this procedure, one often finds that colleagues use their own reading of the text as the sole criterion of whether the description is objective or biassed.

It is admittedly laborious and time-consuming to use a process approach. However, my own study of learners' lexical inferencing skills, i.e. their ability to guess the meaning of unknown words, has yielded insights that justify the efforts involved (HAASTRUP 1991). It is my contention that process studies are necessary as a complement to, or substitute for, a product approach which might easily lead to misguided views, as will be pointed out in the next section.

Misguided views on understanding

This section quotes some widely held views on reading and understanding which are not widely represented in the academic literature today though they are prevalent among teachers, pupils and the general public. If we are to improve text quality, especially in educational texts, we need to change these views. **Misconceived views of reading** are characterized as follows by Urquhart (1993 p. 6):

> a) A text contains a finite amount of information, accessible to all readers. (This information is often equated with "author's message or intended meaning").
> b) The principal aim of the reader should be to extract as much of this information as possible. While it may be necessary for certain purposes to relax the rule, it is usually the case that the better the reading, the more information will be extracted. Thus one type of reading, that which extracts more information, is better than any other type.

In contrast to this view of the reader as a passive recipient, Urquhart emphasizes the receiver's contribution by defining reading as "purposeful interaction with print". (URQUHART 1993 p. 1).

The **method of assessing** what readers get out of a text is of vital importance. Multiple choice questions are often used for this purpose. However, although reading research examines comprehension processes, tests of reading skills are not brought into line with current reading theory, i.e. they lack construct validity and just touch on the surface of readers' understanding. A large international comparative study of students' reading literacy in over 30 countries (ELLEY 1992), placed Denmark at the wrong end of the scale, and has created a much heated debate in this country. Important aspects of the debate are precisely to what extent the assessment procedure in the form of multiple choice questions can be regarded as valid.

Finally, it is a misguided view that **text accessibility** is essential for textbooks ("readers") in mother tongue teaching only. The above-mentioned Danish official report on the quality of textbooks discusses text accessibility in relation to textbooks for Danish teaching, but omits it in the case of textbooks for history, the other school subject under investigation. (Ministry of Education 1994).

Having so confidently distinguished between what in my view are useful and not-so-useful approaches to understanding, I shall address a problem to which there seems to be no immediate solution.

The reader's or the teacher's purpose?

As an introduction to the problem let us keep in mind that successful reading is dependent on the extent to which the reader knows what she wants to get out of her reading experience. The teacher of a class of 14-year-olds has just asked them to study a set text for Friday on the formation of the EEC. Pupil A thinks to herself that she had better concentrate on Danish and English attitudes to Europe, since she knows from experience that it has her teacher's special interest. What is uppermost in pupil B's mind is that she ought to be able to give a brief summary of the text, as her teacher often starts the lesson with this activity. If pupils A and B were asked about their reading objectives, they might not be able to formulate them, but even so their level of awareness is high enough for their reading to have a sense of direction. Finally, we have pupil C, who just reads the text – twice over – but does not consider what she is going to use it for. She just reads.

It is trivial but probably true to observe that what the different pupils got out of their reading was dependent on what they put in. Pupils A and B will be able to carry out the tasks they had set themselves, whereas pupil C will most likely be able to do very little. This is because there is no such thing as "comprehension" or "understanding". What there is, is comprehension of specific aspects of a text, such as the kind of comprehension that is necessary for reporting the text, criticizing the text etc. In short, comprehension has to be qualified as "comprehension of what" or "comprehension for what". Just as we stress a sender's intentionality or purpose, we must not forget the receiver's purpose, or her intention with her reading.

Now, in order to enhance pupils' purposeful reading, many textbook writers produce "study questions" and "points for discussion", and encourage their readers to familiarize themselves with them before they study the actual texts. The same purpose may be served by a workbook accompanying the textbook and containing various exercises.

Along with the individual reader's purpose, and the textbook writer's purpose, there is the teacher's purpose. In the best of situations the two latter go hand in hand, but this is certainly not always the case. As in many other countries, teachers in Denmark value the fact that they have freedom of method in the classroom, and many textbook writers are aware of this. They may therefore be hesitant to write study questions that are too directive; stated positively, they are often at pains to formulate very open questions that allow teachers space and freedom of choice.

Rounding off

I hope it will be agreed that a high-quality text is one that has a well-defined target group for which the text is comprehensible. Furthermore, a high-quality educational text is one that enhances the educational process of which it is an integral part. However, as I have argued throughout, the different partners in the educational process, viz. the textbook writer, the teacher and the individual pupils, may not always have the same end in view.

This is a real dilemma, I believe. Is a good educational text one that suits the reader's purpose? If the textbook writer addresses the pupil directly without relying much on the support of a teacher-led discussion, will the text suffer by being over-didactic? It is, moreover, unrealistic to talk about "a reader"; it is more true to life to think of 24 different readers in a class.

When the Danish official report on textbook quality, mentioned above, addresses the dilemma between textbook dominance and teacher autonomy, the extreme caution with which the authors phrase their recommendations gives support to the idea that this is a highly controversial issue. A case in point comes from their "recommendations" concerning study questions in history textbooks (Ministry of Education 1994). They say that such exercises may be an advantage, if formulated in a very open way, and sum up their recommendations by stating that: "Such study aids do not necessarily inhibit the pupils' initiative and powers of observation" (p. 15) – a rather negative way of phrasing a recommendation!

Hopefully it has become clear from the above discussion that the crux of the matter is not whether a textbook includes study questions or not. In my view the crucial point is the extent to which textbook writers and teachers cooperate in setting tasks for pupils. Textbook writers must bear in mind the teacher's purpose as well as the reader's purpose. The pupil's reading can only be successful if she knows what she is going to use it for; there should, however, be room for the pupil's personal, private reading objectives.

When we want to pinpoint what constitutes a good educational text with respect to readability, we learn best by consulting the pupil and studying her reading processes.

Bibliography

BROWN, A.L. & J.D. DAY: Macrorules for Summarizing Texts: The Development of Expertise. In: *Journal of Verbal Learning and Verbal Behavior 22*, 1983, pp. 1-14.

BROWN, G. & G. YULE: *Discourse Analysis.* Cambridge University Press 1983.

CUMMING, A. et al.: Reading and Summarizing Challenging Texts in First and Second Languages. In: *Reading and Writing: An Interdisciplinary Journal 2*, 1989, pp. 201-219.

ELLEY, W.B.: *How in the World Do Students Read?* The International Association for the Evaluation of Educational Achievement. Hamburg, Grindeldruck 1992.

ERDRICH, L.: *Love Medicine.* London, Futura 1984.

GRABE, W.: Current Developments in Second Language Reading Research. In: *TESOL Quarterly 25:3*, 1991.

HAASTRUP, K.: *Lexical Inferencing or Talking about Words.* Tübingen, Gunter Narr 1991.

MEJDING, J.: *Den grimme ælling og svanerne? – om danske elevers læsefærdigheder.* ("The ugly duckling and the swans? On the reading proficiency of Danish pupils"). Copenhagen, The Danish Institute of Education 1994.

Ministry of Education: *Kvalitet i uddannelse og undervisning. Dansk- og historiebøger.* ("Quality in education and teaching: Danish and history textbooks"). Copenhagen 1994.

URQUHART, A.H.: Draft Bandscales for Reading. (Unpublished manuscript). IELTS Research projects 1993. Plymouth, UK; Marjons College of Higher Education.

Fiction and Faction in Textbooks

Egil Børre Johnsen

When applied to the genre of textbook texts, Ferdinand de Saussure's classical distinction between *langue* (meaning collectively developed, normalized language) and *parole* (meaning more individual or situation/function-specific language) will prompt two types of questions. One type concerns the degree of normality in the so-called ordinary prose of the textbook. The other applies to the special nature of textbook prose, which at one and the same time is a manifestation of scholarship, popularization, educational philosophy, educational method and – possibly – of the author's personality.

Since textbook texts are written for school and educational purposes, it would be difficult to associate their "normality" exclusively with the descriptive ("Textbooks are written in neutral prose"). It would be equally difficult to tie their special characteristics exclusively to the normative ("Textbooks tell what is correct and democratic" (grammar/social science)). In a very special way, textbook texts are conveyors of information and attitudes. Perhaps one might even say that by virtue of their institutional authority, they neutralize norms in a language and within a context which really belong only to the school. This dual nature is also reflected in the fuzziness of the questions posed in many investigations. Several researchers have analyzed textbook language on the basis of specific assumptions about ordinary prose, assumptions which may or may not derive from general theories postulated by language and readability researchers. However, very few have ever written analyses which are holistic in the sense that they simultaneously relate linguistic analyses to patterns for evaluating ordinary prose, to discussions of the special nature of the relevant subject's content and to the textbook genre's extraordinarily large number of different premises.

I would like to refer to Suzanne de Castell's contention (CASTELL 1990) that textbooks are in themselves interpretations of the world and must therefore also be interpreted, as pupils learn to do much earlier with fiction texts. That perspective makes it natural to ask whether it is not new approaches to problems rather than new methods that are needed in the area of accessibility.

Fiction and faction

As an example of such an approach, I propose that we regard educational texts as **literary products**. As a starting point, I choose to distinguish briefly between certain notions concerning "reality" and "literature".

A text is lying if it pretends to present as truth a "fact" which is verifiably not a fact. But there are facts and facts, as well as lies and lies. Thus, a German textbook from 1990 states that

> Überall gibt es Zeugnisse aus der Vergangenheit. In eurem Ort und der Umgebung könnten es sein: alte Gräber, Burgen, Schlösser, Häuser, Strassen ... (NITZSCHKE 1990 p. 28)

Many children grow up in German and European cities to-day without being physically surrounded by memories such as those suggested. The quotation is not in itself an obvious lie. It is, however, one of thousands of examples of the semi-lies constituting the phenomenon of faction. Statements like the one just quoted will be found in most contemporary European textbooks. Eager to arouse enthusiasm and intimacy, authors and publishers are not able to discern between what is and what should be. The result is one which I personally would like to call faction.

The semi-fictional example from my German textbook represents only the half of faction which it is less easy to discern. The other half consists of a mixture of facts and quasi-artistic endeavours, a form of "documentarism" that is perilously distant from documentation. You can find modern textbooks which contain lots of fiction. You can also find page upon page presenting information in the form of irrefutable single facts. However, whatever the intention, equivocation both in vocabulary and structure may render "non-fiction" fictional as well as factional – especially factional. As a total form, in their whole construction, textbooks are essentially and by tradition factional. As indicated above, this is mainly due to their traditional literary role, which is one of the conveyors of the attitudes constituting the national heritage (which, if we look closely, might turn out to be a common European more than a national one).

This factional form of textbooks may be distinguished from fiction in the following way: Fiction is a manifest form of understanding and interpretation. Tradition has long ago established its character; there is a contract telling the reader to be aware and keep awake, as the text may or may not give a true picture of reality: this is for the reader to decide. Texts of faction are, on the contrary, not liable to be read with the kind of critical attention pupils are taught to apply to the *belles lettres*. They are – officially and in real life – considered to be non-fiction. But already the term "non-fiction" is a compromise which has a limited sense. It does express a definite intention. However, recent linguistic and literary sciences have taught us that ontologically speaking, it is virtually impossible to suppose a clear, conscious intention (on the part of the writer) easily and unambiguously transferrable to another mind (the reader).

"Faction" is a new word for an old phenomenon. Researchers unaware of textbooks as literature are, of course, free to speak about "documentarism" as if it were a post-1945 novelty. As students and pupils, however, we have had to cope with it for the whole century. Some of us have done quite well. Others have never managed to break the code.

It's a factional world

How real a world is ours? Last summer there was an advertisement in every underground station in London depicting a beautiful man with a slim body diving into the water. First, he had rubbed his skin with a new type of cream which would enable his body to feel the water better than his skin could by itself. There was only one text, consisting of seven words and running like this: "It's so real it's unreal". When I saw this publicity text, I came to think about schoolbooks: They are so real that they are unreal.

Now, this has always been the case. Textbooks are of course representations of certain idealistic perceptions and would-be-models; they have never been intended as conveyers of fresh analyses. However, this state of things cannot continue, for the good reason that in the

1990s strange things are happening. Adults are gradually becoming child readers, while children will probably have to develop the traditional reading capacity of adults if they are to retain a necessary minimum of rationality or common sense in their perception of the world. I will give two examples to explain what I mean.

In 1993, Simon & Schuster published a bestseller about the life and work of Edward Kennedy. The cover blurb said that the book "presents thoughts and dialogues partly constructed by the author. But these are based upon his profound knowledge of situations and events."

The writer himself, Joe McGinnis, immediately demanded that this text be removed from the cover. In its place he wrote an epilogue where he states: "I have described persons and episodes out of what I have easily been able to conclude on the foundation of Kennedy's general points of views."

Joe McGinnis is a bestselling American author. His book about Kennedy was sold to an important TV-company before it was even published, and I would guess that it has already attained the status of true history in the minds of a public which has studied his interviews with Kennedy – interviews that never took place.

Today, the media tell us the kind of stories that we used to love as children, stories which we can understand. More and more, the newspaper articles tend to be **stories that are well told** – and that is the point. We are gradually being taught to look at the world in the way we learnt to do when we were children: everything that comes to us is real provided we are excited by it. Thus the best-told story, in the press and in so-called non-fictional writing, is most close to "reality". So when Frankenstein one day knocks at your door, you will not ask him if he has escaped from the Carnival. You will know that he is Frankenstein because he comes from the Carnival. Standing there in the doorway, we are the new grown-up children waiting for his story, which had better be fictional (factional?) if it is to be believed.

This notion is now stealthily beginning to gain ground in the world of textbook publishers. It is à la mode to ask for stories, a trend which started several years ago, with books entitled "Teaching as story-telling", "The importance of story" etc. But there are stories and stories; and most textbook stories are still underdeveloped. They go like this:

> The greatest American naval officer was John Paul Jones. He was daring.
> He attacked ships off the British coast. In a famous battle, Jones' ship, the

Photo: Pressens Bild.

"Bonhomme Richard", fought the British ship "Serapis". At one point in the battle Jones' ship was sinking. When asked to give up, Jones answered, "I have not yet begun to fight." He went on to win.

This is taken from an American textbook whose last edition was published four years ago. Some persons still seem to think that story-telling is identical with the mentioning of names. I am afraid there is more to it than that.

Some remarks on a new educational literacy

I would like to propose a single approach instead of several. I would choose to consider textbooks as a form of literary art and would demand that the standard lists of 1001 criteria be forgotten and be replaced by the notion of 'text quality'.

This point of view implies active opposition to certain elementary types of traditional thinking. These are three ways of thinking that can no longer be accepted:

1. The books are written for an institutionally determined purpose and must therefore be "neutral".

2. There must therefore be no author's voice, no metatext in the textbook.

3. Textbooks are to offer true and objective representations of the outside world.

I reject these points. If textbooks are to make any sense today, they must both define and oppose the institution they serve. They must be written by authors and not by teams. And they must show us the truth, namely that textbook worlds are written worlds and not final statements either of what reality is or of what it should be.

We all know, of course, that good texts demand character. I would like to quote Margery Fisher on this point:

> But there is more to an information book than its technical aspect. Each one should contain fact, concept and attitude. Any book that is not a mere collection of facts (and many of them are only this) has an end in view, a generalisation towards which the facts are arranged. This final concept might be a statement of the result of victory or defeat, in a book of historical fact, or the definition of the end-product of a process and its use in a book of technology, it might be the summing-up of the purpose of an institution or a public service, or the pronouncement of an abstract idea.
>
> Behind the generalisation that concludes, or should conclude, an information book lies the attitude of the writer. [...] The enthusiasm of an expert discernible in a book on a sport, a pastime, a hobby, is in itself an attitude. Flatness of style, perfunctory writing, flabbiness in generalisation, all denote the lack of an attitude and promise ill for any book. (FISHER 1972 p. 12)

Story-telling in textbooks has so far consisted mainly of the dropping of names (Per & Kari, Peter & Mary) of protagonists who lack individual features and appear in sterilized scenes. The mere occurrence of such "stories" may wrongly be seen as a warrant for literary quality. But they are of no value unless they are able to cope with professional demands. Jostein Gaarder's book *Sophie's World* is now becoming the classical, worldwide example of what happens when subject matter and real story-telling are perfectly combined.

Story-telling is, of course, by no means the only way to proceed. Awareness of both the problem and its possibilities has been demonstrated by the linguist Marianne Haslev (1975). In preparing a grammar for schools, she wanted to fight the tradition of using arbitrary pattern phrases without meaning. The protagonists in all her examples are animals with certain mutual relationships.

A more serious procedure would be to see all parts of the book as subordinate to one thematically dominating principle. For instance, there is no paragraph in Norwegian curricula planning legislation to prevent a writer of a chemistry text book from framing the entire text within the theme of ecology.

Another way is to use personal presence and metatext. This does not necessarily mean having a "personal voice" or frequent "Hello's"; but the author should be present in a way which systematically and repeatedly demands the reader's responsibility. The reader must be reminded of the intentions of which he is an active part in a constantly ongoing process.

Procedures such as those just mentioned call for accuracy, concentration and consistency throughout the entire text, and the success of any possible stories depends upon these qualities. A popular form is no good unless it reminds the reader of its own limitations. John Ahier (1988) has shown how ambitious demands for both scientific precision and for the 1001 sufficient educational measures resulted in unusable texts and context in British social science textbooks. The texts were written as if there were no conflict of interests between scientific knowledge and the school's subject matter. This is no simplification, but a complication:

> one must acknowledge the conflicting claims of scholarship and pedagogy. [...] there is something of a scandal in the way teachers and texts represented these disciplines in ways which excluded pupils from their uncertainties. What is argued in this section [in Ahier's book] is that, whilst corrections of inaccuracies and misunderstandings (possibly based on historical and geographical research) is necessary, it can only be part of a wider structural analysis along with a consideration of the ways in which the texts produced a sense of reality, regardless of the apparent unrealistic idealizations within them. (AHIER 1988 pp. 61-62)

Glimpses from a success

In my latest textbook, *The World* (JOHNSEN 1992), I have tried to respond to Ahier's criticism. Its preface goes like this:

> This textbook is not history itself. Neither is it geography itself. It is just one out of millions of books written on these topics. And the books have been written by different people who have again been reading what others wrote.

> Imagine a scene so deep that no one can see where it ends. That is history. It takes place in a landscape so wide that no eye can catch it all. That is geography.

> In front of it all there is a curtain stretching right into heaven. No one can remove that curtain. But it is possible to pull aside a flap and have a glimpse. This textbook is such a glimpse.

E.B. Johnsen: Verden. ("The World"). Aschehoug, Oslo 1992.

The book had a double objective:

1. If a story, it had to be a good story – a "real" story.

2. It had to be written in such a way that the students were led to see that all texts, this one included, are interpretations. This insight would have to be conveyed through the reading of the text – that is, by the book itself. This experience is necessary before the students encounter McGinnis on TV or Frankenstein in the gutter.

The World is a detective story, a thriller based upon the hunt for a manuscript and a book. The reader is led in and out of fiction. This is done in a manner that reminds the reader that descriptions of the world are also interpretations of facts and not a presentation of everlasting truth. Reisa is an 11 years old girl who hunts for a manuscript – as does her uncle Vanya. She is always accompanied by her dog Ryk, a so-called "bird-dog", meaning that it is able to fly. And Reisa knows how to get around in the world. Besides, she does not have to attend school. Why not? may you ask. The answer is of course that she has read so many books; she is a literate person, a reading adventurer. So books become a leitmotif in the book.

When adult readers open a book they expect cohesion, a meaning, a thread woven through its pages. Contemporary Western textbooks lack this dimension. Instead, they are trapped by conventions concerning method and extra-textual enhancements: "Everything" has been incorporated or mentioned in the books. Thus the readers perceive nothing. This is why I have tried, in *The World*, to apply the general artistic rules necessary to all good literature, also to that of schools.

One very simple example: the story is full of certain leitmotifs, a central one being that of pyramids. The use of mountains and stones is not an arbitrary one, but is meant to emphasise the notion of stability amidst all the commotion of our long historical past (which is very rapidly sketched in the book).

The book has a few main themes, one of which is this question: What is history? When Reisa solves this problem, she also solves the criminal problem. This happens in the last chapter, during the distribution of the Nobel Peace Prize in our University Aula in Oslo. During the production of the book my editor reminded me that the prize ceremony was to be moved to the Town Hall, and asked me to change picture and text. But I refused. I did not want to be up to date. Instead, I wanted the story to be coherent and fully consistent. You see, there is a painting by

Edvard Munch in the University Aula. Its title is "History". And it is while interpreting this picture that Reisa finds the solution to the crime.

There is, of course, also a students' book full of information, tasks and exercises – all developed in the classroom by three young teachers. The pattern is the same as in the book: its main personalities are all represented, and they speak and think with different voices. There is the girl: she is authoritative; she informs and acts. There is the dog: he cannot talk, so he is the one who reflects. There is the uncle: he has a childish capacity for dreams and imagination.

The World is an international book. The girl and the dog have no national home address and might come from any country. They have been conceived by, and belong to, a European written culture of which we are all part.

Bibliography

AHIER, J.: *Industry, Children and the Nation. An Analysis of National Identity in School Textbooks.* London, The Falmer Press 1988.

CASTELL, S. de: Teaching the Textbook: Teacher/Text Authority and the Problem of Interpretation. In: *Linguistics and Education 2/1990.*

FISHER, M.: *Matters of fact. Aspects of Non-Fiction for Children.* Leicester, Brockhampton Press 1972.

HASLEV, M.: *Setningsanalyse og beslektede emner i syntaks.* ("Sentence analysis and related syntactic topics"). Oslo, Universitetsforlaget 1975.

JOHNSEN, E.B.: *Verden.* ("The World"). Oslo, Aschehoug 1992.

NITZSCHKE, V.: *Politik. Lernen und Handeln für Heute und Morgen.* Frankfurt am Main, Diesterweg 1990.

The Process of a Curriculum Reform

Sten Sjørslev

On the 1st August 1994 a new Education Act came into force in Denmark, introducing new concepts of teaching and learning into the Folkeskole (primary and lower secondary school). Teaching is now to be adapted to the needs of the individual pupil, with an ongoing process of internal evaluation forming the basis for the setting of aims. Subject teaching alternates with interdisciplinary lessons. It is central to these new concepts that the pupils should engage actively and share responsibility for the acquisition and application of knowledge and skills. The teacher is regarded as the one who is responsible for inaugurating, maintaining, stimulating and supporting the learning process, on behalf of both the individual pupils and of the class, which is the basic teaching unit.

The Act also paves the way for a reform of the syllabus, since the Minister of Education is authorised to establish aims and central areas of knowledge and skill (**CKS**) for the individual subjects, and to issue recommended curricula and teaching guidelines. Beyond these primary educational metatexts there lies a primary meta-metatext (see page 172 below) which forms the written basis for constructing the metatextual documents (formulation of aims, central areas, curricula and guidelines). The genesis, formation, application and possible effects of this text will be dealt with in the present article.

Educational texts as administrative documents

There is a tradition in Denmark for school administration to be organised locally; and changes made in the late 1980s in the regulations governing local authority schools involved a further decentralisation, with authority devolving on the local councils and the individual schools to a greater degree than previously. This was effected via legislation under the heading of "Administering aims and framework", which replaced the previous detailed regulations. A similar change in the legislative basis has characterised all areas within the public administration. For schools, this new emphasis has meant a revision of the form of the texts which function as governing documents in relation to the local education authorities and institutions. However, these changes in school administration, with the division of authority between state and municipality, are not the only grounds for reformulating the texts which determine the content of the teaching.

Didactics and textual practice

The didactic principles which were established in the 60s and 70s (GUNDEM 1992), and which formed the basis for the description of teaching content in the school reform of 1975, were largely based on an American conception of curricula in which school subjects are regarded as transformed versions of the corresponding academic disciplines. However, an important aspect of the Danish interpretation of this didactics was that the final determination of teaching content was left for the teachers to make on the basis of their professional experience (NORDENBO, forthcoming). This didactics has since been criticised for not taking into consideration the fact that school subjects have their own "social history" (GOODSON 1984) and also have a different and broader educational purpose than academic subjects. Furthermore, this didactics appears to equate systematic method with the way in which pupils acquire understanding and knowledge – an approach which ignores the pupils' own background and experiences as premises for learning.

Finally, the result of developments, particularly throughout the 1980s, in the drawing up of documents concerning aims, curricula and guidelines have indicated a need to adjust the didactic foundation. Up to 1984, the conception and realization of textual practice were fairly uniform, with a high degree of agreement as to the elements which should be included in a description of aims, a set of recommended guidelines and a curriculum; but from that year a remarkable shift can be discerned.

The legal statuses of the texts differ decisively. Under both the present Education Act and previous ones, it is the minister who is authorised to lay down the aims of the subjects. What is new is that the minister is now also authorised to determine central areas of knowledge and skills, and local authority schools are obliged to organize their teaching accordingly. However, the curricula issued by the Ministry are only recommended suggestions; each local authority must decide whether to accept them completely or partially or to reject them. In practice, the vast majority of education authorities do adopt the ministerial proposals. Finally, the teaching guidelines are of the nature of practical instructions which the teacher can choose to follow, use as inspiration or ignore completely.

Since 1984, however, the statement of aims has increasingly included the kind of specification of content which has traditionally belonged to the curriculum. Teaching guidelines have been extended with sections on central areas of knowledge such as one might expect to find in a curriculum; and from time to time a curriculum will contain elements which were previously placed in the guidelines. The need to establish a new basis for the construction of the texts describing the content of the teaching is strengthened by the fact that the aims, curricula and guidelines of approximately 40% of the subjects have been revised on the same prototype since 1975.

Processes of curriculum formation

A number of partially overlapping processes interact in the drawing up of the descriptions of the teaching content. Firstly there is the process of establishing the basis upon which the curricular texts can be written: the educational text considered below, "Guidelines for describing content in the curricular planning in the Department for the Folkeskole" (**GCC**), is a result of this process.

Secondly, there is the nearly parallel process in which the individual elements – the statement of aims, the CKS, the syllabus and teaching guidelines for the thirty obligatory and optional subjects and topics – are formulated.[1] The results of this process are the primary educational metatexts which function as administrative documents for the municipalities and schools.

Finally there is a third process which presumes that the actors in the schools, primarily the teachers, will put the content of the texts into practice in their teaching. Important criteria for a good educational text must be found in factors which have significance for this realisation of the content of the texts. This issue will be dealt with more fully below.

Some discussions of fundamental issues

From late 1990 until mid-1991 the Ministerial Department for the Fol-keskole set up a discussion group consisting of officials working in the area of school content and persons attached to institutions of educational research and development. The aim of this group was to discuss the principles upon which work on the new curriculum could be based. The point of departure were the developments within didactic thinking and textual practice outlined above. The group drew up a catalogue of problems, in which interest focused on the following questions:

- How is it possible to develop an understanding of school subjects and a related description of individual subjects which takes into account the fact that their content changes continually, and that it should combine with the other subjects taught to form a unified context for the pupils' acquisition of knowledge and skills?
- How can the teaching content best be organized as subjects so as to ensure the interests of the overall educational aim? – And last but by no means least:
- How can the texts be constructed so as to be seen by the actors in the school whose job it is to realize them in practice, as not merely intelligible but indispensable?

When the discussions were over it was apparent that special attention would have to be devoted to the question of the teacher's functional curriculum – that is, the practical realisation of the descriptions of aim and content – in the construction of the curricular texts. There was a need to build bridges between the very general formulations of aims and the specific requirements named in the teaching guidelines. In his suggestions for meeting this need, Hans Jørgen Kristensen introduced the idea of drawing up a "supra-subject" curriculum which would articulate the broader trends in the requirements for the qualifications the pupils are to acquire. There should also be a number of short texts specifying the minimum levels for each subject; and finally, recommended material should be collected in inspirational anthologies describing the various content and method options.

On this hard-won foundation the discussions concerning the structure and content of the curricular planning were continued internally in the Department for the Folkeskole from 1991 to 1993. At the inception of the actual curricular planning in October 1993 a text had been prepared: "Guidelines for describing content in the curricular planning in the Department for the Folkeskole" (GCC).

The basic text for curricular planning

The basic text (GCC) is aimed at the designers of the primary educational texts at the meta-level (statement of aims, CKS, curricula).[2] It has two main sections, with an introduction stating explicitly that the aims, central areas of knowledge and skills and curricula only apply to the individual subjects named in the Act. On the other hand, no statement of aims, CKS or curriculum needed to be written for the teaching in interdisciplinary topics and problems which alternates with the normal subject teaching, as prescribed in the Act. This aspect of the teaching content is reserved for the recommendatory texts which the Ministry also plans to issue as a step in the implementation of the Act.

The text is divided into two sections, since the statements of the aims of the individual subjects and the CKS are prescriptive documents in relation to local authorities, schools and teachers, whilst the curricula are recommendatory in relation to the local authorities but binding for schools and teachers once they have been adopted at the local level. The guidelines are meant exclusively as advice to teachers. The aims and the CKS therefore belong together in one section, and the curricula and guidelines in the other.

However, the two sections have the same structure. In each case there is an introduction explaining the nature of the different texts with regard to their content, structure and range, and this is followed by a list of headings specifying the requirements for the drawing up of the texts. In connection with the statements of aims for the individual subjects, content and form are required to relate to the overall aims for schools stipulated in the Act. With regard to the form, the text says that

a division into three parts corresponding to the overall aims of the Folkeskole should form the point of reference for the discussion and establishment of the aims of the individual subjects.

This text was filled out according to the guidelines for each subject
included in the completed metatext. However, during the process of
creating this type of text there arose uncertainty and disagreement on
one essential point concerning the correct understanding of content
and structure. One important requirement which the GCC makes for
the aims of a subject is that they should include grounds which extend
beyond the subject itself: in other words, grounds found in the actual
subject cannot explain why it is to be taught at school; the subject's very
existence must be justified in terms of the contribution it can make to
the schools' educative task as it is expressed in a very concise form in
the general statement of aims. Several of the first drafts of subject aims
therefore contained introductory remarks concerning the reasons why
the subject was to be taught in schools. These so-called preambles were
often to a greater or lesser extent repetitions of the values named in the

*J.F. Willumsen: Sophus Claussen reading his poem "Imperia" for Helge Rode and Willumsen,
1915. Aarhus Kunstmuseum.*

61

statement of aims for schools, and could also be so general that with a little imagination they could be applied to any school subject. The Department for the Folkeskole therefore decided to revise the instructions on this point and in its place construct a specification of the content of the three parts making up the subject aims.

This specification was expressed by means of questions corresponding to each part. For Part 1 the question is: **What?** What knowledge, skills, working methods and expressive forms make up this subject's contribution? For Part 2 the question was: **How?** How should such knowledge, skills etc. be acquired so as to form a framework for experiences, enterprise and absorption, maintain the pupils' desire to learn and give them confidence in their own opportunities and background as the basis for forming opinions and taking action? Finally, the question to Part 3 is: **Why?** Here a justification should be presented for the answers to Parts 1 and 2; and these answers must naturally correspond to Part 3 in the overall aims of the school, which expresses the underlying values with regard to culture, nature and democracy. With these points in mind, the aims of the individual subjects were formulated.

A new type of text

There were a number of special difficulties involved in the drawing up of guidelines for CKS, as they would have to be used to establish a new type of text and give it its place in a textual hierarchy expressive of a tradition, though one undergoing redefinition. And the establishment of the CKS would give occasion for an adaptation of the form of the adjacent textual types, the statement of aims and the curriculum.

The extreme positions with regard to the concern of the CKS as textual type can be expressed under the headings "Field Concepts" and "Minimum Requirements". In the case of Field Concepts, it is emphasised that content categories should have a high degree of generalisation and abstraction to allow the options for the final choice of content to be as open as possible. In the case of Minimum Requirements, the CKS must be formulated in detail, with an indication of which content elements are the minimum in the teaching of the subject. In the GCC it is the Field Concepts approach which forms the basis for the requirements for the drawing up of this textual type.

Clarifications

However, in the preliminary work to establish CKS as a textual type a new problem emerged: to begin with especially, the formulation of CKS tended to be an extension of the statements of aims. In many cases such phrases as "the aim is" and "what is in view is" are used. Thus it became difficult to discern the intention of the texts as to the content of the central area of knowledge and skills for the respective subjects. Clarifying discussions and a new round of formulation effected a certain purgation, though remnants of the formulations of aims still cling to the completed texts.

In their final form the aims and CKS were collected in an illustrated volume (*Aims and central areas of knowledge and skills. Subjects taught in the Folkeskole*, 1994), and a large edition was issued in August 1994. Every teacher in the Folkeskole has received a copy, and some have also been sent to the schools. It is beyond a doubt that even during their creation these texts have had, and will continue to have, a great influence on the structure and content of the deluge of new textbooks which is expected to flood the schools in the coming years.

GCC and the curricula

At this moment, that section of the GCC which deals with curricula and teaching guidelines is being written in the committees and boards which produce such texts. GCC states that the textual nature of the curricula should be such that in practice they can serve teachers as their most important tool in the planning of their teaching. To satisfy this requirement the texts must be specific and precise as well as spacious and imaginative to enable the teachers, both separately and in collaboration, to visualise the progression and contextualization which should be established throughout the course of schooling. In extension of this general requirement, GCC stresses the fact that the Act requires both the creative dimension and information technology to be integrated in all subjects, and this means that these elements should also be included in the description of curricula.

The good educational text

An educational text of the meta-meta-level, like the GCC, must be evaluated on the basis of several criteria.

Firstly, it should not only have brought the general didactic discussion up to date. It must also attempt to trace future didactic developments by taking a stand on the principle positions manifested in the didactic discussion in recent years or decades.

Secondly, its specifications for the texts it is designed to generate should be so clear that consensus can be reached as to the realisation of their requirements even in a large group consisting of persons whose didactic allegiances vary.

Finally, this primary educational text on a meta-meta-level must also take into account the views of the readers who are to use the primary educational metatexts (see page and below) which will be the result of its influence.

This last criterion for a good educational text has been particularly difficult to take into consideration within GCC, but the first two criteria have also been difficult to live up to. The didactics and self-image of the individual subjects have proved to be strong factors in relation to the first criterion, and partly as a result of this there have also been certain problems in attaining an acceptable degree of agreement concerning the practical realisation of the requirements for the textual structure.

At the time of writing (October 1994) we are in the process of formulating a new description of the teaching content. The trial runs that have been made at organising the writing of educational metatexts have not been entirely successful in all respects. But it will not be possible to evaluate the effect on the content of the teaching which ought to result from the statement of aims, the CKS, the curricula and the teaching guidelines until they have been in use for some years. And the creation of these texts has made it clear that there is in all events a need to follow them up by means of special forms of communication.

Notes

1. Curriculum planning is organised under seven committees supported by secretariat groups for each of the subjects and topics taught in the Folkeskole. Also collaborating are representatives for the teachers' and parents' organisations, academic educationalists and persons from other interest groups. There is also a coordinating committee chaired by the director of the Ministerial Department for the Folkeskole; its members consist of the chairpersons of the seven curriculum committees, specialists in secondary education and representatives of local government and the teachers' union. In all, about 150 people have been involved.
2. The planning of the curriculum was begun towards the end of October 1993. In the spring of 1994, the statement of aims and the central areas of knowledge and skills were formulated, and were issued to the schools in August 1994. The provisional time schedule requires the first version of the curricula to be completed by 1st December 1994: the teaching guidelines are expected to be ready early in the spring of 1995.

Bibliography

Formål og centrale kundskabs- og færdighedsområder. Folkeskolens fag. ("Aims and central areas of knowledge and skills. Subjects taught in the Folkeskole"). Copenhagen; Ministry of Education, Department for the Folkeskole 1994.

GOODSON, I.: Subjects for Study: Towards a Social History of Curriculum. In: GOODSON, J. & S. BALL (eds.): *Defining the Curriculum. Histories & Ethnographies*. Lewes, East Sussex; The Falmer Press 1984, pp. 25-44.

GUNDEM, B.B.: Notes on the development of Nordic didactics. In: *Journal of Curriculum Studies 24:1*, 1992, pp. 61-70.

NORDENBO, S.E.: Danish didactics – an outline of history and research. In: HOPMAN, S. & K. RIQUARTS (eds.): *Didactics and/or curriculum*. (Forthcoming).

Curriculum Analysis: The Example of History

Vagn Oluf Nielsen

In Denmark a curriculum is a political and educational document which establishes the aims and contents of the subject.

In the following I will present a few observations on curricula as educational texts, or rather, in the language of historians, make an analysis of curricula as sources to some essential conditions in the Folkeskole (the Danish public school system). In other words, I will investigate what curricula actually are the sources of and thus what they are not the sources of. An analysis of this kind implies an investigation of the situations in which curricula originate and of their content. In order to limit the analysis and keep it specific I will stick to curricula within history, which is my own subject, and will focus especially on the history curricula drawn up in 1977, 1981, and 1984, appending examples from earlier work on the contents of history teaching so as to ensure a historical perspective.

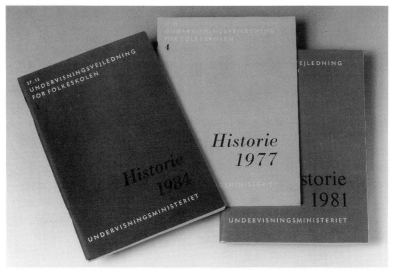

Photo: Niels Elswing.

The concept of a source

It will be necessary to refer to various historical methods and terms in the article's analysis of curricula as sources. The most important ones are explained in this section.

Among these is the distinction between two conceptions of the source, the absolute and the functional. The **absolute concept** involves understanding the source as an absolute statement of the truth of the matter under consideration. The **functional concept**, on the other hand, asserts that it is the question under investigation which determines the specific use of the source. Nowadays the absolute concept has been more or less abandoned; it is the functional understanding of sources which is dominant within modern historical studies.

Related to the functional concept of the source is the methodic distinction between two **inferential modes**. One involves regarding the source as a report: on the basis of the source inferences can be drawn about a part of **reality**. The other inferential mode implies that the source is to be seen as a survival or relic, from which inferences can be drawn concerning the **origin** of the source.

In the case of curricula, there are certain implications. To start with, inferences can be drawn about reality. For instance, the curricula can be read for information about what pupils actually learn at school and how the teaching is conducted. But according to the other inferential mode, deductions can also be made concerning the origin of the source: for instance, about the wishes of the authorities as to how the pupils were to be educated – what children were to learn and how they were to be taught it.

Of these two inferential modes, the latter can be most dependably applied to curricula, which are therefore seen as primary sources to knowledge of the authorities' intentions, and only secondarily as sources to the everyday reality of the school.

The status of the curriculum – then and now

It appears that the concept of the 'curriculum' did not seriously gain entry into Danish educational legislation and theory until after the Second World War. The Education Act of 1899 mentions "Plans of Instruction for the Folkeskoler", and in the subsequent legally binding circular issued in 1900 by the Minister of Education and Ecclesiastical Affairs, Bishop H.V. Sthyr,[1] the aims and contents of the individual subjects were established.

The Education Acts of 1937 and 1958 also require each school to draw up a Plan of Instruction; it is noteworthy that both Acts give the same description of the content of such a plan:

a) whether teaching in the classes is for boys and girls together or whether they are taught separately;
b) hours of instruction in each class;
c) detailed plan of the week;
d) subjects to be taught;
e) aims to be achieved;
f) plan of holidays.[2]

It was not until 1941 that the Act of 1937 was followed up by a Ministerial Order dealing with the aims of the teaching in the Folkeskole. However, in this the Ministry declined to issue a general order about how the subjects ought to be taught as it did not wish to make any "attempts to direct the course of the teaching, as long as the aims described are achieved."[3] Due probably to the special conditions appertaining during the Occupation, only a curtailed Order was issued, and curricula for the individual subjects were not included.

The Public Education Act of 1958 included guidelines for teaching, the so-called Blue Report. Here an account was given of the aims, contents, methods and teaching materials of each subject, and a circular was later sent out restating the aims and making them binding. The Blue Report uses the word "curriculum", stating that the report was made by a curriculum committee set up by the Ministry of Education.[4]

During the 1960s and 1970s the term "curriculum" was used more and more in educational and political circles. This is no doubt due to the fact that interest in didactics grew at the cost of interest in the methodology of teaching and, to some extent, in the structure of the school.

The Public Education Act of 26th June 1975, § 16, section 1, states that "each school is to draw up a teaching plan" which should contain various stipulations about the organization and contents of "the individual subjects, the subject groups and topics, indicated by central areas of knowledge and skills or illustrated by examples (curricula)". This should be seen in connection with § 4, section 5, which states that "the

Minister of Education lays down the rules for the aims of the individual subjects or subject groups, and issues curricular recommendations."[5]

There is a similar provision in the new Education Act of 23rd June 1993 § 10: "The Minister of Eduction lays down the rules for the aims of the subjects and indicates central areas of knowledge and skills."[6] The Act also stipulates that each school is to draw up curricula which can be identical with the ministerial recommendations and must be approved by the municipal council.

Thus it can be established:

- that there is a long tradition for each school drawing up its own teaching plan and curriculum, which must however be approved by a political authority;
- that the ministerial curricula are consequently only advisory, though they are usually adopted by the municipalities, and that they are approved and issued by the Ministry of Education;
- that the term "curriculum" was first clarified after the Second World War in response to an increased interest in the aims and contents of the teaching.

The originators and contents of curricula

When we look back to the years up to and including the Second World War and consider the ministerial circulars and orders concerning the aims and contents of teaching that were issued, we find it characteristic that the documents were actually drawn up by the minister himself in collaboration with a few of his officials, and that there does not seem to have been a great deal of political discussion on their contents. This is true of the Sthyr circular (1900) and the Ministerial Order of 1941. But the increased interest in the aims and contents of teaching which manifested itself after the war also entailed a greater attention to curricular planning. Subsequent to the Blue Report it became normal practice for the minister to set up broadly based curricular committees whose composition might vary but usually included both academic and educational experts and representatives of political and civil organizations. A clear democratization of curricular planning has come about, even though in the last resort it is still the minister who determines the final contents of the curricular recommendations.

In the last 25 years these have come to be presented under the title of "Recommendations for Teaching in the Folkeskole" and to be comprised in three documents:

1. An account of the aims of each subject. This is legally binding for all teachers and pupils working with the subject.
2. Advice and examples which can be referred to in the teaching of the subject. These are only recommendations.
3. A suggested syllabus for the subject. This appears as an appendix to no. 2 even though it is the most important document as it implies the aims and is legally binding when or if it is adopted as the local curriculum for a municipality or school.

In accordance with the new law, present curricular planning has inserted a section after the statement of aims: "Central areas of knowledge and skills". Here the contents of the relevant subject is stated in general terms.[7] Like the aims, this is legally binding for the schools of the whole country, and is clearly added in order to prevent too high a degree of de-centralization. This is given the support of the teachers' union and the Ministry, under the motto "A common school with a local character".

A comparative analysis

This section will present a comparison between recent years' curricula in history. The relation between the contents and the originating situation will be emphasised.

During the implementation of the new Education Act of 1975, Ritt Bjerregaard, then Minister of Education, rejected the history curriculum on the grounds that it called for an approach that was so academic that neither teachers nor pupils would get any benefit from it. The aims were completely changed and a recommended curriculum issued under the title *History 1977*. The aims, which were retained in *History 1981* and *History 1984*, go like this:

> 1. The aim of the teaching is that the pupils acquire knowledge of the life of previous ages, with their conceptual paradigms and social conditions, and that they gain an experience of the relation between past and present and of the changes which have taken place in the opportunities for human display.

2. The pupils should be made familiar with the tradition of Danish social and cultural life which is the foundation for both change and continuity.

3. The pupils should be trained to read and listen to historical accounts and evaluate them as explanation of phenomena outside their own experience.[8]

History 1977

Reading the aims listed above one gets a strong impression that they are based on the ideal of objective knowledge. In paragraph 1, for example, it is stated that the pupils are to "acquire knowledge of the life of previous ages, with their conceptual paradigms and social conditions", but nothing is said about the basis for this learning. There is talk of "**the** relationship between past and present", of "**the** changes which have taken place in the opportunities for human display", and of "**the** tradition of Danish social and cultural life". There is no mention of the pupils investigating and discussing possible relations, changes or traditions on the basis of different historical accounts and sources, nor that they should consider different interpretations. It is true that the last paragraph says that the pupils "should be trained to listen to and read historical accounts and evaluate them as explanation of phenomena outside their own experience", but it is to be doubted whether in this context the word "evaluate" implies that the pupils should consider a variety of accounts and explanations of the same historical phenomena. In such a case the text would have been formulated quite differently. My doubts are substantiated by the Minister of Education's wish to "counteract the tendency to make this subject academic in the folkeskole".

On one essential point, however, the formulation is progressive. It is actually stated that it is desirable for the pupils to "gain an experience of the relation between past and present and of the changes which have taken place in the opportunities for human display". Even though an objectification of the relation between past and present is implied, as mentioned above, the choice of words contains the seed of a historical consciousness, an understanding of which has become central to Nordic ideas on historical didactics in the 1990s.

In its contents *History 1977* lived up to its formulation of aims, but its lifetime was short. In August 1978 a coalition was formed by the Social Democratic Party and the Liberal Party, who issued a document expounding the government's political platform. Point 16 of this document stated that the position of history teaching in the Folkeskole should be revised. In the autumn of 1978 and the winter of 1979 a resolution on changes in the Education Act implemented the restoration of obligatory history teaching in the 3rd to 9th grades and not merely in the 3rd to 7th grades as according to the 1975 Act. In the commentary to this resolution it is stated that this was decided "on the consideration that it is essential to the pupils' understanding of their own times that they should acquire a thorough knowledge of the past and thus be enabled to see the connection between the past and the present."[9] The proposers of the resolution wished to strengthen history as a school subject as a direct extension of point 1 in the formulation of aims with its implicit objectivistic concept of historical consciousness.

In the first debate on the resolution there were few speakers who inquired about the contents of history teaching. When she was questioned on this point at the close of the debate, Dorte Bennedsen, then Minister of Education, could only say that it "had naturally not been discussed by the coalition parties, neither was it the concern of Parliament. It is the business of Parliament to lay down the framework but not the content of the individual subjects. It has not been discussed."[10] However, the spokesman for the Liberal Party, Bertel Haarder, promised to act as an indefatigable watchdog against the powers who would use history lessons for contemporary social studies.

History 1981

In the autumn of 1979 the Minister of Education asked the Education Council for Lower Schools to consider what steps should be taken to meet the parliamentary decision to introduce history as an obligatory subject in the 8th and 9th grades. The Council decided that it was not sufficient simply to make alterations in the section of *History 1977* dealing with history as an optional subject in the 8th and 9th grade but that it would be advisable to draw up a completely new syllabus and guidelines so as to enable history teaching from the 3rd to the 9th grade to be described as a whole. A special commission headed by the Director of the Copenhagen School System, Hans Jensen, was appointed to implement this decision and given a year in which to do so. Like the Education Council, this commission was composed of representatives of various bodies: the Employers' Organization, the Trade Unions, the parents' and the pupils' organizations, the Teachers' Union, the Union of History Teachers and the Royal Danish School of Educational Studies.

In 1980, after an interesting and productive series of negotiations, the commission presented its "Suggestions for the syllabus of teaching in history" to the Minister of Education via the Council for Lower Schools, and in the spring of 1981 this document was issued as *History 1981*.

A vigorous debate on the educational, political and ideological aspects of these suggestions was immediately stirred up in journals and the press. The document was attacked for focusing too much on society and social structure and too little on people. There were some who thought that it was elitist, and would be difficult for teachers and pupils to live up to. A few others maintained that the chronological principle organizing the 6th to 9th grade syllabus was too rigid and would prevent the pupils from perceiving connections between their own lives and those of past societies.

But *History 1981* was attacked principally for being biassed towards Marxism, especially because of its choice of terminology and because it contained the requirement that pupils should also learn to apply the Marxist conception of history. In the final phase of the commission's work the representative of the Employers' Associations had expressed strong reservations on this point.

History 1984

As an ordinary member of parliament Bertel Haarder had joined in the criticism of *History 1981*, so it was natural that when he became Minister of Education in the autumn of 1982 one of his first acts was to appoint a commission to draw up a new set of proposals concerning history as a school subject as an alternative to *History 1981*. In accordance with § 16, section 1 of the Education Act, these proposals were to contain a section on the central areas of knowledge. The new commission had a different composition to the one which produced *History 1981*: its members were appointed by the Minister personally, and the organizations were not represented. In the spring of 1984 the commission presented its proposals under the name of *History 1984*.

In what follows a comparison will be made between *History 1981* and *History 1984*. This will be in two parts, one dealing with the similarities between the two documents and the other with the differences. It should be stressed that the two curricula have the same aims and that the comparison will deal mainly with the two recommended syllabuses and only to a lesser extent with the guidelines for teaching.

Similarities

1. As stated above, both documents have a similar formulation of aims.

2. Each of the documents makes a clear organizational division between history teaching in the 3rd to 5th grades and in the 6th to 9th grades. Work in the junior grades is not tied to a chronological sequence, and both curricula allow for interdisciplinary projects, principally in collaboration with biology and geography. For the senior grades, both curricula call for the contents of the teaching to be organized chronologically, starting with the most ancient periods in the 6th grade and ending up with contemporary history in the 9th grade.

3. Both documents stress national culture and identity. The focus is on the history of Denmark, and this makes up the main contents of the teaching. But they both include the history of the Nordic countries, of Europe and of the world, mainly when these areas provide a necessary background to the Danish history.

4. As stated, both documents emphasise the national history, and both explain this in the same way: that it is important for the pupils to learn about conditions of life through the ages in the area where they themselves are growing up.

5. Thus there is a common understanding in both curricula that history teaching should contribute to the pupils' better understanding of their own lives and of the society they are living in and thus give them a democratic education.

Differences

1. One of the two important differences between the two curricula is that *History 1981* makes a point of stating that when interpreting the

past the pupils should work with divergent views of history, i.e. total conceptions, with the related terms "societal types" and "patterns". And it goes on to state which views of history it means: "Work should be done on conceptions of historical process which regard ideas and great personalities as determining social conditions and change, and on those based on materialism and the conditions of production. It is important that the reciprocal action of the various patterns in society be understood." (*History 1981* p. 44).

History 1984 does not use these terms or propose that pupils do comparative work with divergent views of history. But in several places it mentions "aspects of history" (political, cultural, economic and social, corresponding to the "patterns" of *History 1981*) and states that it is "essential that the various aspects of history are not dealt with separately but are seen as interactive, even if one or more of them are emphasized or taken as the starting point." (*History 1984* p. 71). Unlike *History 1981*, this document says nothing about the possible nature of the interaction.

2. The second decisive difference is that *History 1984* includes a most important section on "central areas of knowledge" to which *History 1981* has nothing corresponding. This section contains a brief account of the major areas of Danish history with glimpses of their interaction with the history of Nordic countries, Europe and the rest of the world – the intention being that these areas should make up "the nucleus of the teaching and be included in the teachers' course plans." (*History 1984* pp. 68-69).

Conclusions

These two essential differences between the two curricula justify one in concluding that whilst *History 1981* aspires to effect a national education in political democracy largely through work with divergent views of history, and thus expresses a conception of history as mainly a tool subject, *History 1984* pursues the same aims mainly by working with central areas of knowledge, and thus expresses a conception of history as mainly a contents subject. But it must be emphasized that both curricula operate with both tools and contents as their basis. Perhaps the situation can be summed up by saying that *History 1981* emphasises "views" whilst *History 1984* emphasises "subject-matter".

There is no doubt that the three curricular commissions had their interior conflicts and that their documents were divergent, nor that these conflicts and divergencies are in part an expression of their origins in the differing views of the authorities and the politicians as to what kind of education Danish schoolchildren ought to have.

Curricula are educational texts which are sources for an understanding of the authorities' views on schooling, their educational attitudes and most profoundly their ideas about the good society and the good life. These days, however, this can be difficult to demonstrate because curricular planning has evolved into such a complicated process with many persons and interests involved. But this does not alter the fundamental point that curricula should be regarded more as "relics" than as "reports".

Notes

1. Cirkulære ang. Undervisningen i de enkelte Skolefag paa Grundlag af Loven af 24. Marts 1899. In: *Love og Ekspeditioner vedkommende Kirke- og Skolevæsen. 1899-1900.* ("Laws and provisions concerning the ecclesiastical and educational authorities. 1899-1900"). Copenhagen 1901, pp. 327-339.
2. *Folkeskoleloven af 18. Maj 1937.* ("Public Education Act of 18th May 1937"). Issued by A. Barfod. Copenhagen 1941, p. 10.
3. Bekendtgørelse om Maalet for Folkeskolens Undervisning. In: *Love og Ekspeditioner vedkommende Kirke- og Skolevæsen. 1941-42.* ("Laws and provisions concerning the ecclesiastical and educational authorities. 1941-42"). Copenhagen 1943, pp. 81-82.
4. *Undervisningsvejledning for Folkeskolen. Betænkning nr. 253, 1960.* ("Guidelines for teaching in the Folkeskole. Report no. 253, 1960"). Copenhagen 1960.
5. *Lov om Folkeskolen af 26. juni 1975.* ("Public Education Act of 26th June 1975"). Introduction and commentary by Henrik Helsted. Copenhagen, Finn Suensons Forlag 1975, pp. 25 and 17.
6. Den nye folkeskolelov. In: *Folkeskolen 28. juni 1993.* Copenhagen, p. 8.
7. *Formål og centrale kundskabs- og færdighedsområder. Folkeskolens fag.* ("Aims and central areas of knowledge and skills. Subjects taught in the Folkeskole"). Copenhagen, Ministry of Education 1994.
8. *Bekendtgørelse af 24. september 1974 om formålet med undervisningen i folkeskolens fag.* ("Ministerial Order of 24th September 1975 on the aims of the subjects taught in the Folkeskole"). Copenhagen, Ministry of Education 1975, § 8.
9. Forslag til Lov om ændring af lov om folkeskolen. Med bemærkninger og bilag. ("Proposals for a resolution concerning changes in the Education Act. With commentary and supplements"). Parliamentary session 1978-79. Copenhagen, p. 2.
10. *Folketingstidende 1978-79. Fortryk.* ("Annals of Parliament 1978-79. Prepublication"). Copenhagen, column 6482.

The Experimental Dilemma:
An Analysis of Textbooks for Physics and Chemistry, and Their Role in Teaching which Emphasizes Experimental Work

Peter Norrild and Helene Sørensen

Physics and chemistry are often characterized by the term "experimental" subjects as new knowledge within the scientific disciplines very often is generated by the interaction of observations, experiments, and theory. The formulation of hypotheses and the following experimental testing has been the fundamental basis for the theoretical development of the subjects for more than two hundred years. Qualitative as well as quantitative experiments have contributed to useful ideas on for example the universe and the elemental composition of matter. In Danish schools physics and chemistry are taught together as an interdisciplinary subject.

As school subjects physics and chemistry have emphasized the role of experiments. But at school experiments are often used in the same way as textreading and problemsolving and virtually never performed with the purpose of creating new knowledge.

The communicative text and prescriptive writings

Textbooks for physics and chemistry often contain two essentially different categories of text: the **communicative**, or factual, type which presents data, theories, models and perspectives, and the **prescriptive** type which gives instructions for performing the experiments which provide the pupils with first-hand experience of using materials, methods of measurement and principles of calculation so that they can acquire the appropriate knowledge and concepts. And these are not meant to be personally formed knowledge and concepts but those that are generally recognised and scientifically authorized.

The important dilemma

Previously, writers of textbooks were not plagued with scruples about the harmony between communicative and prescriptive texts; but the constructivist view of learning and knowledge prevalent nowadays implicitly criticizes the way that the connection between these two types of text has been taken for granted for generations. Constructivism contains the idea that individual pupils construct their own knowledge via a complex interaction between personal experience, cognitive structures, feeling and needs in the actual teaching situation. In other words, even if the connection between the factual communicative text and the prescriptive experimental text is formally designed, there is not much chance that the pupils will form a coherent impression of the book.

Ought there to be exact instructions for experiments with answer sheets for the pupils to report the results which they are expected to achieve? Or should there rather be proposals for investigations and experiments whose aims are so general and broad that there is room for the pupils to participate in planning the details of the organization, working methods and reporting? This is the dilemma for all present writers of textbooks for physics and chemistry.

The didactic choice

The Minister of Education establishes the aims and central areas of knowledge and skill for the individual subjects taught in the Folkeskole, and the Ministry of Education issues a recommended curriculum and a teaching guide as models and aids for the local authorities (cf. Sjørslev and Nielsen above).

There is no tradition in Denmark for the central authorization of teaching material which is produced by commercial publishers and firms. In principle, individual teachers have a large degree of freedom in the way they plan and carry out their teaching, and this includes the freedom to choose their own teaching material. However, for physics and chemistry it is the usual practice to select one textbook system for the whole three years in which this subject is obligatory.

Most textbook systems contain a consistently structured sequence of content with corresponding descriptions of and instructions for demonstrations and experiments. Experience shows that most teachers make thorough use of the books, thus limiting their didactic freedom to the choice of their textbook. In practice the organization of the teaching, with its associated didactic considerations, is done by the author of the textbook.

The book in the classroom

In most physics and chemistry lessons the time is taken up with practical laboratory work. Either the teacher or some of the pupils demonstrate the experiment for the whole class, or else the pupils work in groups, and this work is based on the instructions in the textbook. Sometimes it can remind you of following the recipes in a cookery book. These practical sections are often followed by explanatory passages which point out the implications of the preceding laboratory work. Such passages become incomprehensible if the results of the experiment prove to be different from those predicted, or if for some reason the experiment is not carried out.

At the start of the lesson the pupils are usually told to read through the instructions for the experiment, which might be set out in the textbook or a supplement, or photocopied. The teacher will often go through difficult parts of the recipe with the class, and then small groups of pupils perform the experiment and note down the answers in the question sheet provided. If there is time, the results are reviewed at the end of the lesson. Practical work takes time, especially as the apparatus has first to be got out and afterwards cleaned and put away, so reviewing and discussing the results often has to be left for the next lesson, when the whole business may have become so distant that the pupils are no longer motivated to sum it up and discuss the perspectives of the work done.

Physics and chemistry is an obligatory subject in Denmark from the 7th to the 9th grade. In the 7th grade the lessons are used very largely for laboratory work, and at this level the book mainly has a prescriptive role and may also provide worksheets to be filled in. In the more senior classes more time tends to be used on going through the factually communicative texts, and by the time the pupils are nearing the end of the 9th grade they are expected to be able to read and remember what is in the book. They can choose to be examined in this subject at the end of the 9th grade. The form of the examination reflects the practical, investigative character of the subject in that it consists of practical experimentation together with a conversation on the theory and the perspectives.

Science textbooks in the 1950s

The experimental element was also important in the schoolbooks of forty or fifty years ago. Then, however, there was rarely any mention of suggested experiments or pupils' instructions, but textual and graphic accounts of selected experiments and apparatus. It was very rare that the experiments were performed in class, and the descriptions were so exhaustively detailed that, at least from the authors' point of view, practical work would have been superfluous. This is despite the fact that the ministerial orders of the time and the didactic debate on science in schools certainly emphasized the importance of pupils' own laboratory work.

Texts which describe experiments are difficult to read because without the concrete experience they appear extremely abstract. There is no actual smell, movement, gas or precipitate – just words from an alien, non-sensory world. The drawings are two-dimensional, often floating in a vacuum or perhaps provided with an active hand, and the text gives a variety of details concerning procedure and observations.

In those days it was quite usual that in the examination situation the pupil would have to reproduce on the blackboard or on paper an experiment which they only knew from the book, just as in many Third World countries today physics, chemistry and technical subjects are experimental subjects without the use of a laboratory. Similar texts exist even today, though now the authors often elect to relate the details of an experiment in the form of a cartoon or series of photographs, just as they make a point of "doing" the experiment with "everyday" apparatus such as jam jars, bottles, syringes, etc. In other words, there is a strong tradition for describing experiments which are not expected to be performed in practice.

Learning by doing, and the Sputnik shock

The use of textbooks in the teaching of physics and chemistry underwent a dramatic change at the beginning of the 1970s, both on the basis of the Dewey "learning by doing" philosophy and as a consequence of the Sputnik shock. In England and the USA considerable resources were invested in the development of new teaching programmes with their own textbook systems (SCIS, PSSC, ChemStudy, Nuffield, etc.). In Denmark, these large teaching programmes have a considerable influence on the formation of curricula and teaching guides for schools, and, just as significantly, on the textbook systems which followed in the wake of the curriculum. According to the statement of aims, teaching in these subjects was now supposed to introduce the pupils to "the scientific investigating method", which was defined in the teaching guide as the process by which the pupils collect and classify data, form and test hypotheses and use them to construct theories, models, etc. Now the emphasis was on central scientific concepts, models and methods with universal relevance and application, instead of the multitude of more fortuitous experiences with phenomena and contexts relevant to the everyday life of the pupils.

Gone were the books containing large amounts of text with detailed verbal descriptions of experiments which had to be learnt by heart. Now the pupils were supposed to learn by doing the experiments themselves. The textbooks no longer contained solutions to the exercises (though the teachers' book did, of course). Scientific principles were supposed to be rediscovered! Today one can smile at the influence these theoretical interests had on the didactics of physics and chemistry: the thinking behind it was clumsy and rigid, and did not really focus on the pupils' abilities and needs. The new books with their many laboratory experiments certainly got the pupils active; the only question is, what did they learn?

The level of abstraction

The level of abstraction in the books and the teaching was far too high for the majority of the pupils, and they had difficulty in seeing what the experiments were supposed to show. The textbook authors had care-

3.8 Den elektriske strøms varmevirkning

Strøm kan opvarme en tråd – undertiden så meget, at den
brænder over.

Laboratorie-opgaver

Opgave 1.

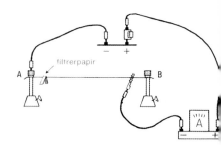

> Sikring, 2 polstænger på fod, 50 cm kanthaltråd 0,25 mm tyk,
> et krokodillenæb, amperemeter, et stykke filtrèrpapir, lednin-
> ger.
>
> 6 V ~

Lav dette kredsløb.

Krokodillenæbbet skal kunne glide frit på tråden, men skal i
begyndelsen være skubbet helt over til B.

Hæng en smal strimmel filtrèrpapir over tråden tæt henne
ved A.

Når krokodillenæbbet nu langsomt skydes hen mod A, stiger
strømstyrken, fordi den indskudte tråd bliver kortere.

Hold øje med amperemeteret.

Udfyld dette skema.

Ved hvilken strømstyrke:	
1) begynder papiret at ryge?	A
2) begynder tråden at gløde?	A
3) brænder tråden over?	A

Opgave 2. Vi laver en dyppevarmer.

> Sikring, 5 cm kanthaltråd 0,25 mm tyk, 2 krokodillenæb, am-
> peremeter, porcelænsskål, termometer, ledninger.
>
> 6 V ~

Lav dette kredsløb.

De to krokodillenæb fastholder hver sin ende af den 5 cm
lange kanthaltråd.

Kanthaltråden holdes ned i en porcelænsskål. Der hældes
netop så meget vand i skålen, at hele kanthaltråden er dæk-
ket.

Hvad viser amperemeteret:

Hvor lang tid tager det at varme vandet op til 50°?

Prøv evt. om du kan få vandet i kog.

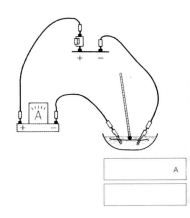

	A

66

E. Flensted-Jensen et al.: *Spørg Naturen. ("Ask nature"). 2nd edition. Gyldendal,
Copenhagen 1983.*

82

Ekstra-opgave

Opgave 3.

> 2 polstænger på fod, 20 cm jerntråd 0,30 mm tyk, et stykke
> filtrèrpapir, amperemeter, ledninger.
>
> 6 V =
>
> NB. I dette forsøg skal du *ikke* bruge sikring!

Sno jerntråden i tætliggende vindinger omkring en blyant.
Træk forsigtigt blyanten ud og lav dette kredsløb.

Hvor højt går amperemeteret op – lige idet du tænder for
strømmen:

A

Hvilken værdi indstiller strømstyrken sig på efter et kort øje-
bliks forløb:

A

Hvorfor falder strømstyrken, når kredsløbet har været tændt
et øjeblik?

Prøv at puste på spiralen. Hvad sker der med strømstyrken,
mens du puster?

Hvorfor ændrer strømstyrken sig, mens du puster på tråden?

3.9. Læs selv. Elektricitet og ildebrande.

Til daglig udnytter vi den elektriske strøms varmevirkning i mange forskellige apparater: strygejern, kogeplade,
dyppekoger, loddekolbe, hårtørrer, osv.
Opvarmningen i disse apparater sker ved, at strømmen
ledes gennem en tråd med stor modstand (et varmele-
geme), mens man sørger for, at tilledningstrådene har
ringe modstand (tykke kobbertråde), så de ikke opvar-
mes noget videre.
Men strømmens varmevirkning kan også være farlig for
os, hvad følgende beretning viser.

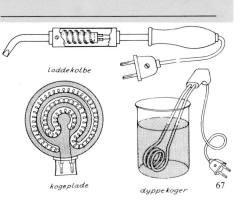

loddekolbe

kogeplade

dyppekoger

67

fully planned a course of experiments which extended over several lessons, but the pupils felt that they knew neither the purpose of the work they were doing nor the rules of the "game".

It is difficult to make the step from specific experimentation to abstract generalization. A 14-year-old working with electrical circuits and measuring the relation between resistance (Ω), current (A) and voltage (V) will not arrive independently at Ohm's Law ($V = \Omega \times A$). But naturally the book can guide the experiment and provide measurement charts and worksheets which are organized so cleverly that the solution appears by itself. Even if Ohm's Law wasn't mentioned before in the book, the pupils realise perfectly well that some results and formulations are more correct than others. And why not get them straight away?

From the mid-70s until well into the 80s the market for science textbooks was flooded with tightly constructed systems which did not leave much initiative to the teacher. Despite exterior differences of layout they all followed the same prototype. This was because the curriculum took the form of a detailed catalogue of topics and concepts, and also because the first system on the market in the mid-70s (*Ask Nature*, published by Gyldendal) became the model for its successors.

The 1980s: physics and chemistry in the spotlight

At the start of the 80s, fear that the technical trades would lack qualified manpower drew attention once more to science teaching in Denmark. Girls were still not choosing scientific subjects in further education, and a large percentage did not enter for the school-leaving examination in physics and chemistry at the end of the 9th grade. And investigations showed that even students studying science subjects in further education gave incorrect explanations for the most fundamental everyday phenomena. "The scientific investigating method", with its great emphasis on general scientific concepts and models, had not been able to clear away their misconceptional and everyday ideas of science.

The detailed curriculum disappears

One reaction to the renewed focus on the subject was that in 1986 a new curriculum and teaching guide was drawn up for physics and chemistry in the Folkeskole. "The scientific investigating method" was banished – almost. The content of the subject was now to be based on familiar materials and phenomena, ideas about the universe, familiar technology and relevant environmental and technological questions. Working methods still comprised a central area of knowledge and skills, but now included a number of very different strategic angles on observation, gathering evidence, use of models, excursions, media, communication etc.

Where previously the curriculum had prescribed precise topics and central concepts and had almost listed them in order, the 1989 curriculum took the form of a number of much more general central areas of knowledge and skills, and the methods of achieving them was left to the teachers and the textbook authors to a far greater degree than previously. One purpose of this more generalized format was clearly to encourage authors and publishers to provide a far more varied selection of teaching material, including thematic material for use in shorter teaching sequences.

Killing off the large, programmed, uniform textbook systems was a way to force teachers to relinquish their slavery to the book and to enter into a situation where they themselves, together with the pupils, would choose the content and working methods, taking into account a number of local variables which included the background, experience and interests of the pupils.

Thus the stage was set for a radical change in the teaching of physics and chemistry. The expectation that pupils and teachers should select the content and plan the teaching together should have resulted in a change of role for the textbook: textbook systems where the order of topics and concepts is determined by the authors ought to have given way to a selection of thematic works.

A majority of teachers, however, still prefer to be guided by textbook systems, perhaps because the idea that there are correct, predetermined ways of learning particular things is deeply ingrained in science teachers, most of whom have received a strongly academic education. Another reason for this preference may be that it can be difficult to structure the topic and theme booklets that happen to be available into a natural educational progression. It might also be that the large textbook systems which are used over and over again are simply the cheapest and simplest option for the school.

New ideas on science education

In recent years, the international debate on science education has stressed the importance of making it possible for the students to become active learners. It is in other words not enough that they are taught the material by a teacher or by conducting experiments according to detailed instructions which allow no space for the pupils' questions or ideas.

The British CLIS project (DRIVER & OLDHAM 1986) gets the pupils to confront their own presumptions and to form new knowledge actively through their work: in other words, to construct their own understanding. In other countries too work is being carried out on projects based on the so-called constructivist theory of learning (NIELSEN & PAULSEN 1992).

One must, however, be on one's guard against simplistic interpretations of constructivist theories of education. It is no easy matter to infer complex relationships from everyday experience or simple laboratory experiments. And it is far from certain that on the basis of a few attempts at experimental work pupils will be able to reconstruct recognised scientific theories which it took centuries to develop, let alone be able to formulate and communicate them (SOLOMON 1994).

The pupils' own work cannot stand alone. It requires knowledge and experience to plan and conduct experiments, and in reality the pupils may need experience with particular working methods and experimental techniques before they can work appropriately with their own experimental investigations. Their work should also be followed up by discussions among themselves and with the teacher.

Even though learning is a very personal matter, individual pupils are nonetheless not isolated in their own cognitive processes. They work in a social context: they exchange experiences, and one idea follows the other. In the dynamic structures that arise in groupwork it is not necessarily scientific argumentation that determines the conclusions that are reached (SOLOMON 1987). Textbooks try both to satisfy the educational wish for the pupils to investigate and experiment, and to provide the desired academic and societal perspectives on physics and chemistry: it may sometimes seem like an impossible task.

The consequences for books

Textbooks for physics and chemistry must necessarily contain different kinds of texts, the narrative, explanatory type and the type which provides factual knowledge and helps the pupils to construct a theoretical framework for ideas. The illustrations in scientific texts often communicate facts in a particularly concentrated way. Typically, the pupils' problem is that they are overburdened with information, or that they can only function in a complex interaction with either the text or the figures. Cartoons are often used in texts designed to initiate pupil activity; otherwise such texts would be heavy and obscure. The very specific instructions can be useful if the equipment which is available corresponds to what is shown in the illustrations, but this is by no means always the case. Illustrations which invoke associations, mood, identification etc. are being introduced in science textbooks, which are starting to resemble books for such subjects as history, with main text, factual grids and illustrations which are both factual and associative. In the future we will also see faction texts in science books. A particular type of humorous illustration, used a great deal in Danish science books in the 1980s to sweeten the pill of boring or irrelevant topics, is now on its way out.

The instructions for practical experimental activities ought to vary in form: some should be structured and prescriptive, whilst others can be open and inspiring, so that the pupils can collaborate in defining and investigating the problem. But open activities are rarely encouraged in science books: it is usually the teacher who suggests them orally.

Influence from other media

In an attempt to simplify complex or abstract subjects, the prose style of many science textbooks is concise, concentrated and "educationalized": no-one is supposed to spot the notion of correctness. These texts can be a problem even for good, practised readers, and consequently some textbook authors have taken over the international journalistic style of popular science magazines such as *Illustrated Science* (Bonnier), which with its vivid illustrations and large passages of text is consumed avidly by many pupils in their spare time.

Authors and publishers of textbooks are also influenced by the gaudy but very deliberate layout of such magazines: they present a supermarket of information, using factual grids, short paragraphs, explanatory cartoons and vivid graphics designed so that to some extent they can be "read" independently of each other. This disjointed but still book-centred lexical style has left its mark on the first generation of electronic multimedia books on CD-ROM, whose original model is often an encyclopedia.

The "non-linear" textbook?

The interactive possibilities of CD-ROM pave the way for individual user availability of information at many levels and in many forms. In future, new CD-ROM products will undoubtedly be far more liberated from the influence of the book. It is natural to suppose that multimedia developments will in their turn have an influence on the forms of books, including science textbooks. They may relinquish some of their linear progression and in return gain qualities better suited to the needs of the individual pupils in an educational culture in which reading is largely guided by what happens in the laboratory where most of the lessons are spent.

Bibliography

DRIVER, R. & V. OLDHAM: A constructivist approach to curriculum development in science. In: *Studies in Science Education 13*, 1986, pp. 105-122.

NIELSEN, H. & A. PAULSEN (eds.): *Undervisning i fysik – Den konstruktivistiske idé*. ("Physics teaching: The constructivist method"). Copenhagen, Gyldendal 1992.

SOLOMON, J.: Social influence on the construction of pupils' understanding of science. In: *Studies in Science Education 14*, 1987, pp. 63-82.

SOLOMON, J.: Constructivism and Quality in Science Education. In: PAULSEN, A. (ed.): *Naturfagenes pædagogik*. ("Teaching science"). Copenhagen, Samfundslitteratur 1994.

The Qualities of Modern Maths Books: A Comparative Analysis

Else Marie Pedersen

> The teacher writes strange things on the board and talks all through the lesson. No-one understands a thing, and everyone is scared to ask questions in case they're called stupid.[1]

This is a typical account of the nightmare of maths lessons. It is quite normal in this subject that the pupils are afraid that they won't understand the material. However, here is the kind of answer one gets when one asks the pupils what good experiences they have had with mathematics:

> You get a great sense of satisfaction when an exercise suddenly comes out right after not understanding anything for a time.[1]

The great euphoria of suddenly understanding something – the aha! experience – is very central to the learning of mathematics. This emotionally powerful experience of understanding – or not understanding, as the case may be – is connected with the fact that in mathematics learning takes place accommodatively. The new knowledge can often not be accommodated to the pupil's existing cognitive structures, and a restructuring is necessary. This is a painful process which many balk at. However, when understanding dawns it is attended with joy.

If the aha! experience never comes mathematics is a lengthy, traumatic business. On the other hand, one such experience can give a "stupid" pupil new determination in her approach to the subject. It is therefore vital that this special way of learning be discussed with the class, so that the pupils will take the preliminary frustrations as a challenge and not be blocked by them.

Affective factors in learning

Accommodative learning which breaks boundaries requires meta-learning and a secure and open environment where the pupils can risk asking "stupid" questions. And the feeling that what is being learnt is important is also an essential affective factor.

Maths is often seen as a subject which gives answers to questions which no-one (no pupil) has asked, and is therefore regarded as pure, meaningless mental acrobatics. It is therefore very important to discuss the questions and the significance of the answers.

On the basis of my experience of two characteristic textbook systems for use in the Gymnasium I will investigate the demands which the specific nature of learning mathematics makes on teaching materials.

Characteristics of two textbook systems

The systems to be considered are:
- Carstensen & Frandsen: *Mathematics 1 for the obligatory level*. Systime 1990 (**C&F**).
- Flemming Clausen et al.: *Numbers and Geometry*. Munksgaard 1988 (**N&G**). And by the same authors: *Analytical Geometry and Functions*. Munksgaard 1989 (**AGF**).

I will focus especially on the areas 8 and 12 of the overall model (cf. below pp. 172 ff.) in my investigations.

Introduction to mathematics

The first encounter with mathematics in the Gymnasium, as it is described in the two systems, is illustrated on pp. 92-93. Where C&F begin *in medias res*, with a definition of a mathematical term, in N&G there is a panoramic introduction which presents mathematics as a cultural activity that has developed in step with the rest of society. The two illustrations touch on this theme: Fig. 1 points out that the distance to the moon and the orbit of the earth cannot be determined without the help of mathematics, whilst Fig. 2 introduces the well of Eratosthenes and thereby the historical aspect of mathematics. Thus the significance of mathematics is discussed.

Introduction of the term "inverse function", AGF

In AGF the term "inverse function" is introduced by means of four simple examples. The first deals with the mail order sale of ecological flour. The price is 8 kr. per order plus 7 kr. per kilo. The price, y, for x kilos of flour can be calculated thus: $y = f(x) = 7x + 8$, as it is dependent on the amount purchased (x). Conversely, it is obvious that the amount one can buy depends on how much money one has. The two functions, the price as a function of the amount, and the amount as a function of the price, are the inverse functions of each other.

This example is elaborated with graphs for the two functions and exercises encouraging the pupils to find similar patterns and use them to formulate a theory about the preconditions for the existence of inverse functions. The mathematical kernel of the topic is presented as the conclusion to these investigations:

> For a one-to-one function $f(x)$, x is clearly also a function of y. This function is called the *inverse function* of y and is denoted as f^{-1}. (AGF p. 21)

The section on inverse functions works well because it takes its departure in the pupils' everyday understanding. By generalising from this and conceptualising actively, they arrive at an implicit understanding of the mathematical concept and can see the point in the exactness of the mathematical terminology.

Introduction of the term "inverse function", C&F

In C&F the concept is introduced thus:

> Let us consider a bijective function $f : A \curvearrowright B$ (Fig. 158). Figure 159 is arrived at by simply reversing the arrow in Fig. 158. We see that a function is also established here, as for each element in A there is a corresponding element in B. This function is called the **inverse** function of f, and to mark the relation with f it is called f^{-1}. (C&F p. 225)

The expression "we see" is characteristic of maths textbooks: it assumes that sender and receiver "see" – in the sense of 'realize' – the same thing at the same point. The pupils who don't see feel stupid, and

J. Carstensen and J.
Frandsen: Matematik 1
for obligatorisk niveau.
("Mathematics 1 for the
obligatory level").
Systime, Herning 1990.

1. Tal og mængder

Mængder

For at skaffe overblik er det ofte fordelagtigt at foretage sammenfatninger og indføre korte, præcise skrivemåder. Således er
"EF-landene" en kort betegnelse for Danmark, Italien,...

Når vi i matematik foretager sådanne sammenfatninger, kaldes
disse for *mængder*. For at sikre, at alle forstår det samme ved
begrebet "mængde", udtrykker vi ved hjælp af en definition (ved-
tægt), hvad der præcist menes.

> **Definition.** En *mængde* er en velafgrænset samling af ting op-
> fattet som en helhed. De enkelte ting kaldes mængdens *elementer*.

EKSEMPEL 1. Mængden bestående af tallene 3, 5 og 7 skrives
kort
$$\{3,5,7\} ,$$
hvilket læses: "Mængden 3,5,7" eller: "Mængden bestående af
elementerne 3,5,7".

Vi illustrerer i reglen mængder ved såkaldte *mængdediagrammer* som
vist på fig. 1. Mængder betegnes med store bogstaver og deres e-
lementer med små bogstaver. På fig. 1 består mængden A af elementerne a,b,c og d, og man skriver

$$A = \{a,b,c,d\} ,$$

9

the ones who do are not given the opportunity to feel clever.

Furthermore, there are a number of passive verbs in this passage
and this makes it heavy and abstract. The mathematical phenomena
seem to proceed under their own steam with no underlying human
activity, and this reinforces the pupils' impression of difficulty. In AGF
mainly active verbs are used.

I am not trying to make the point that the passive voice should be
avoided in mathematical discourse – the nature of the subject would
make this impossible – but that this special language ought to be discussed in class.

Establishing the function f^{-1} by reversing the arrow can sound like
mumbo-jumbo to the pupils if they lack the cognitive structure to relate

1. Geometri

Fig. 1. Jorden er rund, det er klart. I TV ser vi tydeligt ned på vores rundhed fra månen.

1.1 Afstandsbestemmelse

Den kontakt, mennesker nødvendigvis har med den fysiske omverden, giver anledning til en række spørgsmål: Hvad er jorden egentlig for noget? Hvilken form har den? Hvad er solen og månen for noget? Hvad er regn, og hvad er årsag til den? Hvad er regnbuens striber lavet af, og hvad betyder det, når en regnbue optræder på himlen? Hvordan er den blevet til? Osv.

For nogle mennesker dukker spørgsmålene måske op i barndommen, måske senere. Andre opdager muligvis aldrig, at der er noget at spørge om, fordi svarene blev givet af forældre eller andre, før spørgsmålene blev stillet.

I enhver kultur har man på et givet tidspunkt haft sine svar på spørgsmål som de nævnte. Og selve måden at svare på har igen været bestemmende for, hvilken type spørgsmål der blev formuleret. I den vestlige kultur har man blandt andet spurgt om tings og genstandes form, størrelse og indbyrdes afstande. Hvor stor er jorden? Er den rund eller flad, eller har den en helt tredje form? Hvor store er himmellegemerne? Hvor stor er afstanden til solen? Hvor højt er bjerget? Hvor langt er der til kysten? Hvor stor er afstanden mellem to givne byer? Osv. Svarene kan man i dag finde i et leksikon. De hører med til nutidens fasttømrede viden. De serveres med en sikkerhed, der gør enhver tvivl overflødig og udelukker enhver undren over, hvordan man er nået frem til dem. Men hvor kommer egentlig al den viden fra? Hvordan måler man afstanden til solen? Hvordan finder man jordens omkreds?

Vi ser i dette afsnit kun på, hvordan man tidligere har skaffet sig svar på sådanne spørgsmål, der kan karakteriseres med ordene: Hvor langt væk? Hvor højt? Hvor stort?

Det er de færreste af den type problemer, der kan løses ved direkte måling. Man kan ikke måle jordens omkreds med et måle-

Fig. 2. »Eratosthenes' brønd«. Eratosthenes vidste, at solen står lodret over Syene den 21. juni, thi netop på denne dag kaster brønden ingen skygge.

9

F. Clausen et al.: Tal og geometri. ("Numbers and geometry"). Munksgaard, Copenhagen 1989.

it to. The fact that they find it difficult is not made present as a problem. There is nothing to suggest why we should consider a "bijective function" (in T&G this is called a one-to-one function), and the exercises and examples do nothing to prompt the realisation that bijectivity is an absolute **precondition** of a function having an inverse function.

Most pupils, in fact, skim over this central premise, seeing it as simply a case of boring, pedantic formalism. The two following examples illustrate the formal consequences of the definition. They show **how** it is used, but say nothing about the significance of inverse functions. "So what?" is a typical response from the pupils.

This type of mathematical text nourishes a tendency towards an instrumental style of learning,[2] as the pupils' attention is drawn to the way the problem is solved but not to what its nature is.

The formula for solving a quadratic equation

In C&F p. 45 we are told to convert a quadratic equation thus:

$$ax^2 + bx + c = 0 \Leftrightarrow$$
$$4a^2x^2 + 4abx + 4ac = 0$$

The process is described as purely mechanical: "Multiply each side by 4a". There is no clue to why this should be done: actually one could just as well have divided by a. It is never asked why this particular method has been chosen, and the result is that the text appears closed off. The pupils get the impression that mathematics is worked by magic words, and they feel stupid because they would never have got the idea of multiplying by 4a themselves. Their attitude to this formula is typically "I have to learn it by heart".

N&G (pp. 101-102) introduces this topic by means of an authentic and simple example, showing how the Bagdad mathematician Al Khowarismi approached the calculation of area in 825. The problem and the attempts at a solution are clear, and this gives the pupils self-confidence and motivates them to come to grips with quadratic equations in general. And the example has an exotic element which rouses their curiosity and reminds them that mathematics is a historical process.

Pupils' reactions to these two systems

I have used both of these textbook systems in teaching, but did not find that either of them functioned optimally. With C&F the pupils complained that there were too few concrete examples to illustrate the point or meaning of the work they were learning. With N&G and AGF they complained that there were too few examples of the **method** for them to use as models when they were doing their homework. It is true in general of the examples in N&G and AGF that they can be hard to follow because they are heavy on content: as well as following the mathematics the pupils also have to think about phenomena from other subjects, especially history, physics and biology.

Another characteristic of N&G and AGF is that the mathematical content is couched in a wordy prose which puts the subject in a wider context. A frequent result of this is that the pupils find it hard to see what they are actually supposed to do. With C&F it is quite the opposite: here the mathematical "kernels" are always emphasised graphically; but the price of this clarity is that the mathematics can appear to be an isolated construction which the pupils have difficulty in seeing the point of. C&F also deal with the historical and cognitive aspects of mathematics, but only in a few chapters unconnected with the rest of the book.

Neither of these systems discusses the actual learning process.

The role of the teacher

It can be rewarding to use C&F in teaching because the pupils are so grateful for the help one gives them to understand the work. Here it is necessary to show them the historical, social and cognitive context of the formal mathematics; whilst with N&G and AGF one has to distil the pure mathematics from its context and provide routine examples.

One important reason for pupils' negative reception of N&G and AGF is that experience has often taught them to regard maths as a subject with a lot of predesigned formulas and proofs that have to be learnt by heart, and they expect to find formal examples of the use of formulas and exercises to match. When they see the amount of prose the reaction is almost always an exclamation, sometimes joyful, of "This doesn't look like maths!" N&G is based on the pupils' understanding of the world around them, whilst C&F relies on their school experience of mathematics.

Thus when one draws up the criteria for a good educational text one must take into account **the teaching situation** of which it forms a part.

The good educational text

I had expected that N&G and AGF would prove to be the ideal educational text, because it discussed the significance of mathematics and prompted the pupils to learning by doing. But I ended up with the paradoxical situation that the "good" book was hard to teach from, whilst it was easy to use the "poor" book. And the pupils were also least dissatisfied with C&F.

On the basis of my experience with these two systems I conclude that in general 'a good educational text' must:
- be based on the pupils' everyday experience as well as on their school experience;
- discuss the questions which mathematics seeks to answer, and the cognitive significance of the answers;
- give the pupils real opportunities for active, independent concept formation so that their activities are not reduced to an instrumental application of theory;
- emphasise the mathematical kernels graphically, so that they don't vanish in a mass of prose;
- construct an appropriate learning process, from the formulation of problems by means of examples and counter-examples giving implicit knowledge, to the explicit formulation of what has been learnt, and finally to consolidation and application;
- use clear language, so that as far as possible the matter meant is in agreement with the matter taught and learnt. It should be a matter for discussion if the discrepancy is great.

The good educational text should also:
- stimulate curiosity and self-confidence, and avoid "stupidity-markers" such as "we see";
- put emphasis on metacognition so that the pupils can be aware of and attentive to their own individual learning processes.

It is possible to imagine a system consisting of two parallel books, one treating the content in the manner of C&F and the other in the manner of N&G and AGF. It would be the teacher's job to ensure a secure learning environment so that the "dramatic tension between the learning strategies of the pupils and the teaching strategies of the teacher" can create a dynamic, exciting and fruitful situation.[3]

Notes

1. This is taken from a questionnaire which I always give my new maths class at the start of the course.
2. Defined thus by S. Mellin-Olsen:
   Instrumentalism can also be defined as a learning strategy derived from a meta-concept of understanding as instrumental understanding. The learner aims for rules, not for relations and structures. Instrumental understanding can thus be seen as a symptom of some deeper structure, instrumentalism. (MELLIN-OLSEN 1981 p. 351).
3. Ole Skovsmose in BJØRNEBOE et al. (eds.) 1988 p. 69.

Bibliography

BJØRNEBOE, J. et al. (eds.): *Matematikundervisning. Demokrati, Kultur, Højteknologi*. ("Teaching mathematics: Democracy, culture, high technology"). Århus University Press 1988.

DORMOLEN, J. van: Textual analyses. In: CHRISTIANSEN, B. et al. (eds.): *Perspectives on Mathematics Education*. Dordrecht, D. Reidel 1986, pp. 141-171.

MELLIN-OLSEN, S.: Instrumentalism as an Educational Concept. In: *Educational Studies in Mathematics 12*. Dordrecht, D. Reidel 1981, pp. 351-367.

Primary Sources as Educational Texts

Sven Erik Nordenbo

I. Introduction

With the appearance of *the Executive Order on Teaching in the Gymnasium, No. 694, of 4th November 1987* (cf. NORDENBO 1988 and 1989), philosophy was introduced into the Danish Gymnasium (Upper Secondary School) as an optional subject. In the first (and so far the only) curriculum to be drawn up for the subject in the following year, it is required that primary sources ("primary texts") should form the core of the material upon which the concluding examination is based (*Philosophy: Executive Order and Guidelines.* Copenhagen; Ministry of Education, Directorate for the Gymnasium 1988, paragraph 5.2).

From a didactical point of view it can be difficult to understand the reasons for this. According to the curriculum, the primary sources can be taken from a broad period of time stretching from classical antiquity to the present, and many of them contain formulations and ideas which present difficulties that are not simply attributable to the historical circumstances of their origins but are also due to the special nature of this subject. Philosophical primary texts, in short, make great demands on the reader's knowledge and intellectual ability, and this no less true of those that have been canonised as classics.

Why is it a requirement in this subject, and, as will be seen below, in some of the other subjects taught in the Gymnasium, that the pupils should work with primary sources when an adaptation or a textbook is a simpler way to teach the content of the subject? Why use a primary source as an educational text when by its nature it is certainly not that? In short, what is the educational significance of using primary sources as educational texts?

At the yearly meetings between the National Adviser for Religious Education and Philosophy and the philosophy teachers the question of what is to be understood by a primary text has been constantly broached without any clarification being attained. The only agreement reached has been that "textbooks are not primary material", apparently implying that all other texts can be, and that a truce should be declared on the matter. With this negative definition of the concept 'primary texts', the aims of the requirement in the current Executive Order that primary sources should be used in teaching are understandably unclear.

It is therefore of interest to investigate the aims and content of the individual subjects and in connection to this the role of primary sources. This will be carried out in the following way. First, the various types of primary sources referred to in the Executive Order will be identified and a typology established. In order to understand more precisely the intention of the expressions "primary text" and "primary literature" a clarification of these terms outside the educational context will be attempted, and it will be demonstrated that there is great terminological uncertainty about the terms "primary literature", "secondary literature" and "tertiary literature". Following this, the possible didactical interpretations of these expressions will be highlighted, and it will be shown that in an educational context at least two interpretations of primary sources can be made. These correspond to two theories of education (German: *Bildungstheorien*): one from an epistemological point of view and one from a viewpoint of the theory of science and value theory. The article concludes with a summing up which argues for the second interpretation, i.e. viewing primary sources in an educational context characterised from the viewpoint of the theory of science and value theory.

II. Primary sources in the Executive Order on the Gymnasium

A reading of the current Executive Order and Guidelines for Philosophy in the Danish Gymnasium (= *Executive Order for Gymnasia etc., No. 319, of 19th May 1993*) shows (a) that some subjects require primary sources to be used both in teaching and as the basis for examinations, (b) that a single subject requires the use of primary sources in teaching alone, and (c) that primary sources are not mentioned in connection with the remaining subjects, cf. Table I. See p. 100.

With a few exceptions, such as Geography, Social Science, Japanese and Psychology, the rule is that primary sources are required reading

Table I: Primary sources as examination requirement in upper-secondary school subjects.

Primary sources required	Primary sources required only in lessons	Primary sources not required
Visual Arts (paragraphs 7.6 & 7.7)	Religious Studies (paragraph 3.2)	Biology
Danish (paragraph 15.1-2)		Computer Science
Design (paragraph 4.5 b)		Information Technology
Drama (paragraph 4.7)		Business Economics
English (paragraphs 5.2; 12.3; 14.2; 26.3 & 28.2)		Physics
Film and TV Studies (paragraph 4.9)		Physical Education and Sport
Philosophy (paragraph 5.2)		Japanese
French (b paragraph 9.2)		Chemistry
Geography (paragraph 4.6 & 9.6)		Mathematics
Greek (paragraph 5.2)		Science
History with Civics (paragraph 6.3 1))		Psychology
Italian (paragraph 9.2)		Technology
Latin (paragraph 3.2; 8.2 & 14.2)		
Music (paragraph 5.2 & 10.2)		
Classical Studies (paragraph 4.2)		
Russian (paragraph 9.2)		
Social Science (paragraph 4.2 & 10.2)		
Spanish (paragraph 9.2)		
German (a paragraph 11.2; b paragraph 9.2)		

The references in brackets refer to the paragraphs in which the requirements are formulated in the Executive Order of the individual subjects, cf. *Executive Order on The Upper-Secondary School, Upper-Secondary Level Courses and the Sngle Subject Upper-Secondary Examination. (Order on Upper-Secondary Education)*. Copenhagen, Danish Ministry of Education 1994, Supplements.

in language and art subjects but not in scientific and technical subjects.

What kind of primary sources are actually implied in the left and middle columns of Table I? If one extracts all the sentences in the Executive Order which include some expression denoting 'primary sources' but exclude the meaning 'scientific experiment' and then conducts a systematisation of the expressions used, a typology can be drawn up in three main groups.

The first group contains all the forms of primary sources which are not primarily concerned with a language text: e.g. "sculpture", "drawing", "monument", "ceramics", "costume", "slides", "photograph", "video", "film", "theatrical performance", "music", "sound-tape", "computer programme". The second group contains the expressions used to denote primary sources which are either literary, such as "genre", "prose", "novel", "poetry", "drama", or related to the syllabus, such as "work", "teaching material", "reading-list", "standard page", "source material", "supplementary text". Finally, the third group contains the expressions which in various respects qualify the terms "text" or "reading of texts". It should be emphasised that these three groups include all the expressions actually used in the Executive Order for the Gymnasium.

The first group scarcely contains any surprises. Music and Classical Studies are traditional subjects; but the widening of the Gymnasium curriculum to include such new art-related subjects as Visual Arts, Design, Drama, and Film and TV Studies, has meant that an increased number of non-linguistic primary sources need to be used in teaching. It is largely the terms of these subjects, with computer terms as a marked exception, which appear here.

As mentioned above, the second group contains two types of expression, syllabus-related ones like "material", "reading-list" and "page", and text-related ones like "genre" and "literature". It is noteworthy that the expressions "primary literature" and "secondary literature" are not used in such a way that they correspond unambiguously to terms like "fiction" and "non-fiction"; in the Executive Order "non-fiction" is characterised as both "primary literature" and "secondary literature".

The third group can be divided into three sections, cf. Table II. See p. 102.

The first section is characterised by expressions which in some way relate to the term "primary text". The second section is related to the term "non-fictional text". The third section is related either to the circumstances of the text's production or to its educational value with regard to the pupils' presumed previous knowledge of a given text, or lack of the same.

Tables I and II indicate the extension of the term "primary source" (all things to which it applies) when it is used in a didactical context,

Table II: Schematic outline of expressions applied to 'primary text' and 'reading of primary text' in the Executive Order on The Upper-Secondary School, Upper-Secondary Level Courses and the Single Subject Upper-Secondary Examination. (Order on Upper-Secondary Education). Copenhagen, Danish Ministry of Education 1994, Supplements.

Texts	Forms of expression in language			
[Section I] Primary texts Original texts	Texts that are representative			[Section II] Account
Texts that are classical	Imaginative Literature	Drama Drama of Shakespeare	Texts of a theoretical nature	
	Non-fiction texts			
Philosophy Technology Plato	Art history	Cultural history Mathematical texts in foreign languages	Science	
[Section III] Texts that have not been simplified or adapted		Unseen texts *[ukendt tekst]*	*[ekstemporal-tekst]*	
Connected (Latin) texts		*[læst tekst]*	Syllabus texts	
Journal article	Biography	Interview	Essays	
Texts in translations	Adapted text	Paraphrased text	*[tillempet tekst]*	Fabricated (Greek) text

Danish terms not translated directly into English in the official English version of the Executive Order and guidelines are indicated with square brackets and written in italics.

but do not say anything about its intension (all the properties that must be possessed by every particular to which the term can be applied). The following section will investigate whether examining the expressions "primary literature" and "primary text" in a general context can be of any help on this point.

III. Primary sources and source literature

One remarkable and rather surprising result of a search of the expression "primary literature" or "primary text" in national and international databases is that it yields no result. There is apparently no general research on this theme. It is similarly thought-provoking that in none of the guidelines in the Executive Order for the Gymnasium where the expression "primary literature" or "primary text" is used is there any definition of the term. Thus the problem seems to be quite untouched, both within the field of general didactics and of the analysis of educational texts. With regard to the latter area, an investigation of anthologies has been carried out, but the question of the purpose of primary sources as educational text was not directly touched upon (cf. JOHNSEN 1993 pp. 36-40 & 371-373). Attempts to define expressions which seem related to the terms "primary literature" and "primary text" have only been made in a library context.

In a study of *Document typology, illuminated by communication theory,* Birger Hjørland sets up a typology of non-fictional texts (HJØRLAND et al. 1991 pp. v-xxx). Within the category "Document types" he distinguishes between "Treatise literature", "Source literature" and "Survey literature". Of treatise literature it is stated:

> Treatise literature can be defined as the literature that constitutes a line of work as academic, i.e. which contains its fundamental research results. [...] Treatise literature serves as the primary documentation of scholarly knowledge. It is therefore often called *primary literature* [my emphasis]. [...] In non-academic occupations such as art, crafts and industry the literature is not itself the end product – that must be the actual works of art, the artifacts or other manufactured products – and in this case the treatise literature is something secondary. (HJØRLAND et al. 1991 pp. xvii-xviii)

Of source literature it is stated:

> Treatise literature is based on the study of the subject's proper object. The "sources" which different disciplines draw on vary widely. The data or sources of science are mainly experiments and observations of nature itself. In history and other humanistic subjects, written sources may dominate. In cultural studies, it is the cultural processes and products which mainly constitute the source basis of the discipline, etc. (Ibidem p. xviii)

Finally, survey literature is defined thus:

> The function of survey literature is to summarize, simplify, communicate

> the results and insights of treatise literature. Survey literature can for instance take the shape of a handbook or an encyclopedia. (Ibidem p. xxii)

According to this classification, textbooks are classed as survey literature (cf. HJØRLAND 1994 pp. 20-22). In a section of the same work, "Definitions and Lexicon of Terms" (HJØRLAND et al. 1991 pp. 1-107) there are entries under "primary literature", "secondary literature" and "tertiary literature". The entry for "primary literature" gives a cross-reference to the entry for "treatise literature" with subsidiary references to "secondary literature" and "tertiary literature" (ibidem p. 79). The entry on "secondary literature" emphasises that the expression can have a variety of meanings. In biographical works, "primary literature" can be the writings of an author, whilst works about an author are referred to as "secondary literature". In this significance, an author's primary canon is the source literature upon which the treatise literature of secondary authors is based. In scientific subjects bibliographical literature is sometimes referred to as "secondary literature", whilst literature with synthesizing or consolidating functions is sometimes called "tertiary literature". In the humanities the term "secondary literature" can be used about survey literature, and treatise literature will then be called "primary literature", and registration literature (bibliographies, etc.) referred to as "tertiary literature" (HJØRLAND et al. 1991 pp. 86-87). The entry for "tertiary literature" calls it: "A term used by some bibliographers with a meaning which covers certain parts of what we define as survey literature" (Ibidem p. 97). It is not surprising that the authors of this lexicon of terms conclude:

> [...] of the very varied usage of the terms primary, secondary and tertiary literature which is documented here, it is recommended that they be avoided or at least that extremely clear distinctions be maintained between the different meanings. (Ibidem p. 87)

As demonstrated above, this recommendation has in no way been followed in curricula which refer to primary sources in the Danish Gymnasium. These seem to rely on a tradition where the meaning of "primary source" is implicit. We can therefore not transfer a general understanding of the expressions "primary literature" and "primary text" to the didactical context but must directly attempt to uncover their possible didactical meaning.

Immanuel Kant: Kritik der reinen Vernunft. 2nd edition, 1787. Photo: The Royal Library, Copenhagen.

IV. Primary sources in nomothetic and idiographic subjects

In section II it was stated that the three main groups of primary sources are established on the basis of a compendium of all the sentences in the Executive Order for the Gymnasium which mention some form of primary source which is not covered by the phrase "scientific experiment". The distinction made in Table I between subjects which require the study of primary sources and those that do not has been set up on the premiss that a scientific experiment cannot be regarded as a primary source. This premiss is not completely uncontested. In connection with history teaching H. Glöckel writes that

> So wenig guter naturwissenschaftlicher Unterricht ohne Schülerexperimente denkbar ist, so wenig kann der Geschichtsunterricht auf Schülerarbeit an Quellen verzichten. ("Just as good Science teaching is unthinkable without the pupils doing experiments, History teaching cannot do without the pupils working on historical sources."). (GLÖCKEL 1979 p. 185)

If historical sources exemplify "primary sources" it can be maintained that scientific experiments are also a kind of primary source. If we accept this point of view the consequences will be that in principle there is no difference between subjects whose study requires primary sources and those where it does not, because all subjects then require the consideration of primary sources.

But there are other views on primary sources than Glöckel's. The Neo-Kantian Wilhelm Windelband makes a distinction between sciences and history as these two areas of knowledge differ methodologically. Science looks to the typical whilst history looks to the individual. Science seeks for general laws whilst history describes phenomena in their particularity. On this foundation Windelband draws up the now classic distinction between nomothetic and idiographic subject areas. About this distinction he says:

> [D]ie Erfahrungswissenschaften suchen in der Erkenntnis des Wirklichen entweder das Allgemeine in der Form des Naturgesetzes oder das Einzelne in der geschichtlich bestimmten Gestalt [...]. Die einen sind Gesetzeswissenschaften, die anderen Ereigniswissenschaften; jene lehren was immer ist, diese was einmal war. Das wissenschaftliche Denken ist [...] in dem einen Falle nomothetisch, in dem anderen idiographisch. ("To grasp the nature of reality, the empirical sciences seek out either the general in the form of natural laws or the individual in its historical manifestation [...]. One part of the empirical sciences is the study of laws (*Gesetzeswissenschaften*), the other the study of occurrences (*Ereigniswissenschaften*); the first teaches what is always the case, the second what was one time. In the first case the empirical scientific thinking [...] is nomothetic, in the second, idiographic."). (WINDELBAND II 1924 p. 145)

According to Windelband, the knowledge of the humanities (*Geisteswissenschaften*) is the most important since it is by experiencing the particular that people gain access to values.

It can be maintained that in reality it is Windelband's distinction which lurks behind the division of subjects in Table I between those which require the use of primary sources and those which do not. This supposition can also explain the ambiguous position of Geography, Social Science, Japanese and Psychology:

In the Executive Order the description of Psychology reveals the wish to characterise it as a nomothetic subject. Social Science alone is placed among the subjects requiring primary sources simply because it is stated that "non-textbook material" should be included in the works on which the examination is based, but otherwise it is described, like Psychology, as a nomothetic subject. A subject like Geography, on the other hand, contains historical elements and consequently has an idiographic side. Modern languages at an elementary level have an interesting special position. In this respect the position of Japanese in the Danish Gymnasium is comparable to that of French, Italian, Russian, Spanish and German. In the descriptions of these five language subjects the expression "primary sources" only appears in the form of "primary literature" in connection with "the Long Paper" (written in the third and final year of Gymnasium in Danish, History or one of the pupil's optional advanced subjects, cf. *Executive Order on teaching in the Gymnasium*, paragraph 8.1). Otherwise the guidelines for these languages at the elementary level only mention texts as either "adapted" or "unadapted". A level of proficiency which enables the pupil to read "literature" thus seems to be a precondition for the relevance of primary sources. It is therefore the subject's literary content rather than the nature of foreign language teaching which requires the use of primary sources to actualise the subjects' idiographic elements. Finally, in the case of Religious Studies, to the extent that it is regarded as a subject that describes religions as social phenomena it has, like Social Science, a nomothetic character; but it approaches the idiographic when the focus is on the textual foundations of a given religion.

That the alternative interpretation of primary sources suggested here can also be found in didactics is shown by some writings of Bodo von Borries on the topics "source work" and "document analysis":

> "Quellenarbeit" oder "Dokumentenanalyse" ist in vielen Schulfächern eine gebräuchliche Methode, so besonders in Geschichte, aber auch in Politik [...], in Geographie [...], in Religion (etwa Quellenbücher zur Kirchengeschichte) oder in der Philosophie (etwa Auszüge aus "Klassikern"). [...] Es scheint, daß "Quellen" und "Dokumente" in den anderen Fächern vorwiegend für "geschichtliches Erkennen" gebraucht werden und daß in Analogie zur "historischen Arbeitsweise" auch die Auswertung andersartigen Materials (Luftbilder, Interviews) als "Quellenarbeit" bezeichnet wird. ("In many subjects "source work" (*Quellenarbeit*) and "document analysis" (*Dokumentenanalyse*) are an applicable teaching method, in particular in History, but also in Social Science [...], in Geography [..], in Religious Studies (e.g. source books in Church History) or in Philosophy (e.g. excerpts from "the classics"). [...] It appears that in other subjects "sources" and "documents" are mainly applied to advance "historical knowledge" and that in analogy to "historical methodology" the evaluation of materials of another kind (aerial photographs, interviews) is descibed as "source work"."). (von BORRIES 1985 p. 555)

In contrast to Glöckel, von Borries's view, with its emphasis on "historical methodology", represents an interpretation of "primary source" along the line of the one given above in connection with Windelband.

V. Primary sources, didactics and development

Thus in the context of didactics there are at least two possible interpretations of the expression "primary source":

(1) One based on a parallel between "historical sources" and "teacher and pupil experiments", and
(2) one based on the distinction between nomothetic and idiographic studies.

Looking at the matter in more detail it can be said that Glöckel's view is based on a theory implying that the material which can function as the sources of historical and scientific knowledge takes on the same character, due to its very function, as the knowledge it inspires; whereas Windelband's distinction between nomothetic and idiographic studies indicates a qualitative difference on the basis of the kinds of interest which make us pursue them. Another way of expressing this is that Glöckel's concept of a primary source is founded on epistemology whilst the interpretation based on Windelband's distinction is founded on the theory of science and value theory.

These two views of primary sources have their separate implications. The parallel based on epistemology implies that the main function of primary sources is to be adapted for use in a particular subject, whereas the distinction based on the theory of science and value theory sees primary sources as opening the way for a special type of cognition, the knowledge of value. It is therefore reasonable to assume that these two views imply different didactical conceptions of the aim and methods of a Gymnasium subject and the role which primary sources will play in it.

It seems apposite to give an interpretation of the two views of the role of primary sources in the context of theory of education (*Bildungstheorie*), inspired by the systematics of Wolfgang Klafki (cf. KLAFKI 1963 pp. 25-45). The epistemological interpretation sees primary sources, primary literature and primary texts together with other primary sources such as experiments and other empirical data as material which is necessary if the pupils are to work with the professional methods of the respective subjects. This view is consequently related to formal theories of education (*Formale Bildungstheorien*), more specifically to the theory of education in methods (*Theorie der methodischen Bildung*).

In contrast, the interpretation of primary sources, primary literature and primary texts, based on the theory of science and value theory, emphasizes that the use of primary sources can lead to an encounter with certain values. These are found primarily in the humanities (*die Geisteswissenschaften*). Consequently this view is related to the material theories of education (*Materiale Bildungstheorien*), more specifically to the theory of education in the "classics" (*die Bildungstheorie des "Klassischen"*).

If the connection suggested here, between the two interpretations of the didactical role of primary sources and the theory of education in methods and of the theory of education in the "classics", is correct, the didactical consequences are interesting:

For the interpretation based on epistemology one primary source is no more important than any other. The only requirement is that they should be able to form a basis for teaching the subject's methods. From this point of view a primary source is simply an example or representative of a typical case. A literary primary source is not in itself an expression of value but simply an appropriate "source material" for an education in methods, i.e. a means to impart knowledge about and ability to handle literary texts.

In contrast, the interpretation of primary sources based on the theory of science and value theory will only apply to the humanities (*die Geisteswissenschaften*), where primary sources, literature and texts are used because by their very nature they represent or give access to values. From this point of view the selection of a primary source cannot be made simply on the basis of the source's usefulness as exercise material but must necessarily assume or imply that the primary source possesses an intrinsic value.

We are now in a position to give an answer to the question: What is the educational intention in using a primary source as an educational text when by its nature it is not an educational text? According to the interpretation of primary texts based on epistemology, primary texts are used in education as source literature to bring about method development in the pupils. Primary literature and primary text can therefore be used as teaching material for this education in methods and as tools to evaluate the extent to which such education in methods has been effected. But it does not seem necessary that primary sources should be used for this purpose. Other material, including textbooks, could be used.

According to the interpretation of primary texts based on the theory of science and value theory, the educational use of primary texts is to act as the primary source for effecting a development in the pupils such as is theoretically formulated in the theory of education in the "classics". By their very nature, primary literature and primary texts are unavoidably necessary, because they possess either intrinsic value or are the only possible source of the values aimed at. For these reasons the curriculum must require the use of primary sources in teaching and examinations.

VI. Concluding summary

The aim of this article has been to investigate the educational intention of using primary sources in the Danish Gymnasium. It was first ascertained that the use of primary sources is especially required in language and art subjects but not in technical and scientific subjects. It was then demonstrated that a study of the usage of the terms "primary literature" and "primary text" outside of an educational context will not bring us closer to understanding their application in the context of didactics. If we turn directly to the study of primary sources in the context of didactics it can be shown that there are two possible interpretations of their educational intention, one based on epistemology and one on the theory of science and value theory. If these interpretations are placed in a context of didactics it can be shown that they relate respectively to a theory of education in methods and to a theory of education in the "classics". Since primary sources can be useful, but not necessary, for the acquisition of an education in method, whilst they are by contrast necessary in an educational theory concerning "the classics", and as the Executive Order only requires the use of primary sources in quite specific subjects, there is good reason to assert that the point of using primary sources as educational texts should be sought in an interpretation of primary sources based on the theory of science and value theory in an educational context.

It is worthwhile emphasizing that this interpretation of educational primary texts has definite consequences for the theory of the curriculum. The criteria for deciding whether a primary text should form part of the syllabus are based on whether it can be rightfully claimed that the text possesses an intrinsic value or gives access to values. In contrast, the criteria for a primary text in the interpretation based on epistemology would be its possible usefulness or effectiveness as a means of training in method. Therefore the two interpretations of primary sources as educational texts have markedly different didactical consequences.

In conclusion, it can be established that since Philosophy as a subject in the Danish Gymnasium requires the use of primary sources ("primary texts") to form the core of the material upon which the examination is based, the curriculum of the subject must be founded on an interpretation of primary sources which is based on the theory of science and value theory and is consequently connected to a theory of material education, more specifically to the theory of education in the "classics".

Bibliography

Executive Orders and curricula

Bekendtgørelse om fagene m.v. i gymnasiet, nr. 694, af 4. november 1987. ("The Executive Order on teaching in the Gymnasium, No. 694 of 4 November 1987"). Copenhagen, Ministry of Education 1987.

Filosofi: Bekendtgørelse og vejledende retningslinier. ("Philosophy: Executive Order and guidelines"). Copenhagen, Ministry of Education 1988.

Bekendtgørelse om gymnasiet, studenterkursus og enkeltfagsstudentereksamen, nr. 319, af 19. maj 1993. ("The Executive Order on the upper secondary school, upper-secondary level courses and the single subject upper-secondary examination, no. 319 of 19 May 1993"). Copenhagen, Ministry of Education 1993.

Executive Order on The Upper-Secondary School, Upper-Secondary Level Courses and the Single Subject Upper-Secondary Examination. (Order on Upper-Secondary Education). Copenhagen, Ministry of Education 1994.

Books and articles

BORRIES, B. von: Quellenarbeit. In: LENZEN, D. (ed.): *Enzyklopädie Erziehungswissenschaft, Band 4.* Stuttgart, Klett-Cotta 1985, pp. 555-564.

GLÖCKEL, H.: *Geschichtsunterricht.* Bad Heilbrunn, Julius Klinkhardt 1979.

HJØRLAND, B. et al. (eds.): *Faglitteraturens dokumenttyper, –kategorier, medier, –former, –genrer, –niveauer & –kvaliteter.* ("Document typology, –categories, –media, –types, –genres, –levels & –qualities"). 1st provisional edition. Copenhagen, Danmarks Biblioteksskole 1991.

HJØRLAND, B.: *Dokumenttyper og brugergrupper i materialevalget.* ("Document typology and consumer groups by choice of material"). Copenhagen, Danmarks Biblioteksskole 1994.

JOHNSEN, E.B.: *Textbooks in the Kaleidoscope. A Critical Survey of Literature and Research on Educational Texts.* Oslo, Scandinavian University Press 1993.

KLAFKI, W.: *Studien zur Bildungstheorie und Didaktik.* Weinheim & Basel, Beltz 1963.

NORDENBO, S.E.: Philosophieunterricht in Dänemark. In: *Zeitschrift für Didaktik der Philosophie,* 10. Jahrgang, 1988, pp. 247-253.

NORDENBO, S.E.: *The Teaching of Philosophy in the Upper Secondary Schools in Western Europe.* Copenhagen, The Danish National Institute for Educational Research 1989.

WINDELBAND, W.: *Präludien. I-II. Aufsätze und Reden zur Philosophie und ihrer Geschichte.* Tübingen, Mohr 1924.

Using Photographs in Foreign Language Teaching

Marie-Alice Séférian

Pictures have always been used in teaching. A visual representation helps the pupils to see things before their inner eye, and to understand and remember them. Correlation between picture and text is an important element in any educational text as it gets both cerebral hemispheres to work together. Pictures speak to the imagination; they can have a humorous element and can appeal to the human need for play and laughter. When they are beautiful they also appeal to the aesthetic sense and to the senses and the emotions. Pictures have a clear role to play in foreign language teaching, as they often render translation unnecessary.

As soon as the photograph became a normal form of depiction it made its entry into all kinds of educational texts; and in the last decades photographs have become more and more dominant in everyday life, especially in newspapers, magazines and advertising. In most cases they are accompanied by a text. Their purpose can be to awaken or hold the reader's interest, to testify that something really occurred, or to break the monotony of the written text, to provide entertainment. Photography is a technique which everyone can master, and at the same time it is also an art form. A photograph can be just as much a source of aesthetic experience as a painting can, and it can say as much about the creator of the image as about the object depicted.

The development of photography has naturally made its mark on the educational texts used in foreign language teaching, in line with developments in the didactics of the subject. Most emphasis was previously put on the language and only various objects were depicted, but now the interest has shifted to introducing pupils to the foreign culture at the same time as they are learning to communicate in its language. More and more photographs are therefore used in the textbooks, which makes them more attractive and can give a "genuine" picture of the foreign society (people, homes, sights, landscapes ...).

The authors (and/or picture editors) select the pictures which they think typical and which help the pupils to form an impression of the country. Thus the photographs are part of the knowledge the pupils have to acquire when learning a foreign language, and they also correlate with words and sentences to promote linguistic proficiency.

Four beginner systems

To approach the subject concretely, I will first take a glance at some books designed for teaching French in Denmark. All four are aimed at beginners, i.e. 14-15 year-olds, as since 1987 it has been possible to start French as the second foreign language in the 7th grade, or as a third foreign language in the 8th grade. What they have in common is that they are all translated or adapted from a third country: *Formule F* (1987) and *Chouette* (1994) were first issued in Sweden in 1981 and 1991 respectively, *Tricolore* (1988) was first issued in England in 1980, and *On y va tous* (1991) was first issued in Holland in 1988 under the title *Allons-y tous*. They are all lavishly illustrated with photographs and drawings.

Many of the photographs show famous buildings such as the Eiffel Tower or typical landscapes such as a vineyard. These may serve as illustrations and be integrated into the French text. But often they are simply designated with the name of the building or a caption in French. Shops are a favourite motif, especially the baker's, where the text is simply "Voici une boulangerie". The picture is used to teach vocabulary, and to give the pupils an idea of how a French bakery looks.

There are also pictures of people, often youngsters of the same age as the target group. The reader learns very little about these people, sometimes only their names; and they are not met with again later in the book. *Tricolore* is an exception: here the same family appears all through the book. We are told a little about their home, their clothes, the color of their hair etc., but we do not learn who they really are, what they feel and think. In *Formule F* there is an attempt to place a portrait in a more realistic context: above a picture of a young woman sitting at the wheel of a taxi there is the sentence: "Voici Christine Martin. Elle habite près de Bruxelles. Elle est chauffeur de taxi. Christine n'est pas mariée. Elle est fiancée à Philippe, qui est facteur. Ils sont très amoureux. Philippe a un chat mais Christine n'a pas d'animal." (p. 18). The correlation between text and picture can only be called slight. We are shown neither Philippe nor his cat, and there is nothing in the picture to suggest that it was taken in Belgium. Furthermore, nothing more is heard of Christine and her fiancé.

In *On y va tous*, people are often in communicative situations and the text consists of their fictional dialogue. This book is distinguished from the two first by its numerous colour photographs. They are often vividly reproduced, with characters stepping out of the frames and similar devices. There are also two stories told in photographs (p. 14 and p. 19). Two pages (p. 4 and p. 8) represent a photograph album. The pupils are from the start encouraged to look at the pictures: "Look at the pictures carefully. In that way you'll learn a lot about France and be given a lot of extra vocabulary." (p. 3). *Chouette*, the most recent of these four beginner systems, is completely in colour. The layout is more regular than in the other three – duller, some might say. The drawings are all by the same person, which gives the book a uniform appearance. The colours certainly make the book more appetizing, but only in a few places do they enhance the meaning. The correlation between text and pictures is poor. There is for example a chapter called "Henri Carron, reporter" (pp. 38-39) illustrated by the following photos: a newspaper stand (where?), a jet plane taking off with a mountain range in the background (where?), and an express train with a lovely field of yellow mustard in the foreground. We do not know whether the man standing in front of the newspapers with his back to us is the said Henri Carron, who is otherwise telling about his life in the first person. It would have been perfectly natural to show him whilst he was talking.

All in all, these four primers make use of photographs in order to give a realistic all-round picture of France. But as they are not dated, the pupils get a static impression of a foreign society and their historical consciousness is not aroused or increased. A clear tendency to use more, better and larger colour photographs has emerged in the course of the 80s and 90s. Many of the pictures resemble those in tourist brochures (after all, France is very popular with Danish holiday-makers), and their content often gives a stereotyped view of France and the French. Furthermore, the pupils are given very few opportunities to exercise their linguistic and cultural competence in connection with the pictures, and there is little appeal to their imagination.

The Mind's Eye

The Mind's Eye, published in 1980, is quite different. The material, which is not designed for any particular age group and can be used in both mother tongue and foreign language teaching, consists of two books, one for the pupils and one for the teacher. The pupils' book is a collection of photographs (with a few drawings and cartoons) with questions and suggestions for activities. The photographs, most of which are black and white, are selected with a view to their didactic and aesthetic value. Many of them are ambiguous and can thus stimulate the learners to discuss, fantasize and create their own texts. The activities are very varied and encourage both oral and written creativity, putting the learner in the centre. Conversations are supposed to take place between the learners, who are asked to make hypotheses and personal interpretations and invent stories on the basis of the pictures. The texts which follow the pictures often provide the linguistic material that the learners need. The activities suggested are open and are more in the nature of games than of exercises.

As an example one can look at this photograph by Martin Shallcross where the text says:

> 1 Working in pairs, try first of all to imagine what lies beyond the frame of the picture [...]. Consider these questions:
> - What is the fence made *of* and what was it made *for*? [...]
> - Do you think the man is alone? [...]
> - Is he looking at something static or something moving? [...]
> Now change partners and discuss your different views on the picture. [...]
> 2 Now return to your first partner. Look through the book and pick out five other pictures [...] which, taken together with this picture, would make up a story. (MALEY et al. 1980 p. 25)

It is interesting that here the photographs are regarded as pictures; unlike in the primers, which say "Voici une boulangerie" or "Voici Marie", inviting the learners to regard the pictures as if they were real and not allowing distance to be established.

The material as a whole gives opportunities for teaching which appeals both to the imagination and the logical faculty, since the pupils often have to present their own arguments for their personal interpretations. Since many of these pictures are mysterious in so far as one

A. Maley et al.: The Mind's Eye. Cambridge University Press 1980. Photo: Martin Shall-cross.

cannot immediately see what they represent or make out what the characters depicted are doing they arouse curiosity and give free rein to verbal inventiveness. As well as the purely linguistic profit that can be gained from working with these pictures they also teach observation of detail and attention to the world's multiplicity and the subjective nature of representation.

Another advantage in using this material is that it allows the teacher to make selections from among the pictures and activities on the basis of the pupils' interests and linguistic ability. It is also possible for the learners to choose which pictures they wish to work with and justify their choice in the foreign language. The teacher may also be inspired to look for other pictures, take his or her own photographs and construct similar activities. The use of photos can thus be integrated into communicative language teaching which can also be differentiated. The one drawback to the photographic material in *The Mind's Eye* is that no information is given as to when and where the pictures were taken. This is designed to enable free interpretation of the images, which is a good thing, but the disadvantage is that they cannot be used either to give knowledge about English-speaking societies or to train the pupils in social observation.

Selection of photographs

On the basis of this brief examination of four beginner systems and *The Mind's Eye* I will now propose a few suggestions concerning the selection and use of photos in foreign language teaching. Financial considerations are of great importance in choosing teaching systems which have to be purchased in class sets. There is no doubt that colour pictures are more appealing to young people than monochrome, but they raise the cost of the books without appreciably increasing their utility. It may be sufficient to use colour photographs only when colour is necessary to the meaning: to show, for instance, that letter boxes are yellow in France and buses are red in London, or to teach the different flags or discuss the symbolism of colour. Otherwise there is no disadvantage in using black and white pictures as long as they are good, with exciting composition, strong contrasts or fine nuances and an interesting content. Since young people today are bombarded with col-

ourful and exciting pictures in magazines and advertising it is just as
well if teaching books do not try to compete. It is better to aim at pro-

Paris. E. Boubat and M. Tournier: Vues de dos. Gallimard, Paris 1981.

viding a few good pictures. Learning to look at a photograph with a unified content and idiom has its own educational value: pictures of artistic quality give pleasure and personal enrichment.

If the intention is to increase the pupils' ability to concentrate and train them in picture analysis whilst they improve their language proficiency it will be necessary for the books to use comparatively large photos. Furthermore, the correlation between text and picture should encourage written production which goes beyond mere description. A poem or some other kind of literary text used together with an exciting photograph can prompt the learners to speak or write about their experience of the picture. Another way to encourage the learners to produce texts in the foreign language and to see the real world with new eyes is to present them with pictures of well-known buildings or landscapes seen from an unfamiliar angle. Take, for example, this photograph of the Eiffel Tower as seen by the French photographer Edouard Boubat. It is accompanied by a text by the French author Michel Tournier which starts like this: "Paris? Mais c'est la Tour Eiffel! dit la chanson. On est moins loquace au sujet des détritus [= rubbish]".

When one is getting to know a foreign society the first impressions are of enormous consequence. Photographs in primers make a greater impact than the text as they can be understood immediately and are felt to be authentic. So authors and picture editors must be scrupulous about the image they produce of the language area they are dealing with. It is important that the pupils are not given a cliched impression of the foreign country and that their historical consciousness is aroused.

Self-activation

The Mind's Eye can inspire teachers to suggest a variety of activities to promote the pupils' self-activation. A good activity for beginners is to make a fictional family album using pictures cut out of advertising brochures or magazines with captions in the foreign language. Large photostats or slides, either from the publishers or home-made, can be used to supplement the book. Just as writing one's own texts can teach one to be a better reader, so can doing one's own photography help one to understand photographs. An example of a meaningful activity in connection with exchange visits is for a class to produce a brochure with photos and texts about themselves and their town or region to send to the class they are going to meet. Journals of the trip illustrated with photographs which the pupils themselves have taken can be produced by pupils in groups. It is now possible to make good photocopies of pictures, also in colour, so that the travel journals can be duplicated and distributed to the parents. Another creative activity which can encourage interdisciplinary collaboration is using slides to illustrate a talk.

The use of photos in teaching has indubitably great motivational potential, but it requires good books. However, good books are not enough. We know that teaching material can be used in a variety of ways and that its value depends more on the attitude of the teacher than even on the content. Both teachers' books and in-service training ought therefore to emphasize a more varied use of photos in foreign language teaching. This is completely in keeping with the Danish tradition of encouraging pupils' self-activity and giving them opportunities to tackle creative and practical activities.

Bibliography

Beginner systems

BRANDELIUS, M. & I. SUNDELL: *Formule F 1*. Copenhagen, Munksgaard 1987. (Danish adaptation by H. Duschek & E. Kambskard).

HONNOR, S. et al.: *Tricolore 1*. Copenhagen, Grafisk 1988. (Danish adaptation by K. Lauritsen & A.S. Christensen).

LANDGRAAF, W.: *On y va tous 1*. Copenhagen, Haase & Sons 1991. (Danish adaptation by K. Thyregod & B. Vejleborg).

WINBLAD, M. et al.: *Chouette 1*. Copenhagen, Gyldendal 1994. (Danish adaptation by K.J. Andersen & U. Bøyesen).

Other references

BOUBAT, E. & M. TOURNIER: *Vues de dos*. Paris, Gallimard 1981.

MALEY, A. et al.: *The Mind's Eye*. Cambridge University Press 1980.

Youth Culture
– Towards New Educational Texts

Susanne V. Knudsen and Birgitte Tufte

We are in a school in the 1990s, in a small suburb. It is close to a church and built of solid brick, and from the outside looks like a throwback from the 1950s. But behind the entrance lies an enormous single-storey school almost resembling a barracks, and inside there is much evidence of vandalism. All in all, the school gives a signal of **the past, the present, rupture** and **multitemporality**.

Twenty-six 8th grade pupils of both sexes are having a lesson in the mother tongue. They are a mixed bunch, all different sizes, skin colours and backgrounds. The pupils and the teacher have agreed that in some of these lessons they will work with music videos, and the material is not to be chosen by the teacher. So the pupils have brought some of their favourite music videos to the class.

Martin and David have brought one from MTV (Music Television). David gets it started, and twenty-six 14-year-olds watch and listen. Some drift over to one side of the classroom, sit down on the floor and sing along silently to the rap-text. Others dance gently around in time with the rhythm. Some sit at their ease, leaning back critically, distancing themselves. The first two groups are made up mainly of boys, some with hip-hop caps and light brown skins. The group which distances itself from the proceeding is mainly composed of girls.

The title of the video is "Doggystyle", with images from an American ghetto. There is hip-hop dancing and pictures of garbage tips and backyards. The music is pop and rock, overlaid with the singer rapping. Suddenly the singer, his girlfriend and his buddies are changed into dogs which tear around furiously and threateningly. The rap emphasizes the way people can suddenly turn into brutes.

The teacher is a woman of 45. Dressed casually in jeans and a T-shirt she observes with interest the pupils' different types of body language and the non-verbal rupture between the admirers and the opponents of the music video. When the music stops the teacher stands up, takes a piece of chalk and asks the class "Which environment does the video take place in?"

It is now the turn of the pupils who sang along and moved to the rhythm of the music to lean back and distance themselves, whilst the ones who observed critically while the video was playing now come into their own. "It takes place in the Harlem slums". "Yes", says the teacher, satisfied, and the analysis proceeds in the formal tradition, where a text is analyzed on the basis of 'time', 'place', 'environment', 'action', etc.

The pupils who chose the video apparently do not want to contribute to the discussion. They are perfectly familiar with the music video as genre, they understand its imagery and know the rap text by heart. They probably chose this one because they wanted to initiate the other pupils, especially the more bookish ones, and the teacher into a culture which they like and are proficient at.

The teacher has shown her good will by allowing the pupils to bring a music video; but she teaches in the same way as always, and the pupils who usually make verbal contributions also do so now.

Several cultures and two generations clash that morning in the modern school by the old church in the city suburb.

The cultures of school and leisure

The example above is rooted in the culture of the Danish Folkeskole, one of whose aims is education for democracy, with such concepts as **'participation'**, **'joint responsibility'**, **'rights and duties'**, **'intellectual freedom'** and **'equality'** playing a central role.

But these very terms signal that there are several types of culture at stake in Danish schools. "Participation" and "joint responsibility" indicates that the pupils should have a say in determining the content and form of their lessons. But with "duties" there is an implicit intimation of being under obligation: that the pupils should be brought up to recognize specific duties and that the teacher should fill the empty vessels with knowledge and attitudes.

However, what these school cultures have in common is that they focus on **verbal texts**. They are based on the book: the textbook. In the

1970s there was a relaxation of traditional practices when new forms of text such as comic books, advertisements and popular literature started to be used in the classroom. The concept of the text was broadened and could now be defined as both verbal and non-verbal. Thus such forms as pictures and films could be used as texts in teaching. But the teaching was still based on the humanistic tradition of education which distinguishes between quality texts and substandard texts. Furthermore, the traditional methods of literary criticism were applied to this **extended textuality**. The emphasis was on the message, and no account was taken of the characteristic aesthetic and expressive dimensions of the texts.

These days, the culturally significant texts are not just books and quality texts but to a large extent pictures and music; and children and young people take a particular interest in them. TV, videos and music provide them with shared out-of-school interests; the new cultural forms have a function for them both on the level of the group and of the individual. On the one hand the media culture is exclusively concerned with selling products and lifestyle to the young; on the other, in a world of change and disruption kids are looking for models to identify with in the figures, environments and expressive forms of the media. Their knowledge of media culture is extensive; they know all about TV series like "Beverly Hills", music videos from MTV and the numerous innovations within TV commercials.

14-year-olds today participate in a number of leisure cultures which we would classify as **youth cultures**. In other words, there will be some pupils in a class who identify with the hip hop culture whilst others are into heavy, techno, pop etc. The concept of extended textuality makes it possible for these various youth cultures and their expressive forms to be used in teaching.

Youth Cultures

In Denmark, **hip hop** is a modified form of the original American underground culture, an Afro-American protest against oppression, racism and violence. In Denmark hip hop is mostly about parties, love

Photo: Sonja Iskov/2. maj.

and colourful experiences, though its themes now and then are violence and racism. According to the young, there are various trends within hip hop: "hardcore", with hard-hitting anti-racist and political messages in music videos, rap and rock music; "wannabes" are whites who would rather be blacks; "smooths" never declare their opinions and avoid confrontations, musically, they prefer blues, pop, jazz etc; "weekend" hip hoppers meet in front of the TV and on the dance floor. The costume that distinguishes hip hoppers consists of caps worn backwards, wide trousers, shirts and boots. They hang out on the streets, and their graffiti and tags are seen everywhere in the larger towns.

Heavy in music means hard rock, also called "heavy metal" and "concrete-rock". The subheadings are "speed" (very fast rhythm) and possibly "trash" (dead metal with aggressive music and texts dealing with violence and death). "Heavies" dress in tight jeans, belts with rivets and pointed boots. They festoon their T-shirts with stickers showing exploding skulls and skeletons.

Techno uses technology to splice the music on tape. The trademark of this kind of music is an endlessly repeated rhythm. The technos hold large parties where one of their practices is to drink milk to enable them to dance into a trance without taking drugs. Their clothing might consist of black plastic bin-liners.

House is pure dance music which originated at private parties. The melodies are catchy, and the music can be played very quickly. The style is liberated, a mixture of 1960s hippy and 1970s disco. The clothing is loose shirts and wide trousers.

Finally, the cultures of football, horse-riding, etc. occupy a large part of the leisure time of young people. Many participate in several youth cultures and can rapidly shift allegiance.

Strong feelings can be involved in the choice of a youth culture. A hip hopper, for example, might say "hip hoppers hate heavies". In general, allegiances seem to be chosen on the basis of temperament, gender and social background.

Force fields

There are thus two major cultures, of **school** and of **leisure time**, and each includes several subsidiary cultures. There are school cultures that point in different directions, and there are leisure cultures upon which commercialisation, lifestyle and the media have increasing influence. On the one hand the culture of the school provides an opening for working with the pupils' own experiences and interests, including the youth cultures. On the other hand, the schools guide the pupils in the direction of learned skills with the accent on the verbal approach.

In the daily life and consciousness of children and young people these two major cultures interact and have a mutual influence on each other. In school they learn skills and attitudes which involve knowledge and values. From the media they receive experiences and another type of knowledge, and they work through emotional and moral questions. A force field exists between the cultures of school and of leisure.

Most teachers belong to a generation which grew up with the printed media as the primary field of education, and with a conception of the mass media as phenomena which usually have no place in education, though they might have limited uses: a film can be a teaching aid in biology lessons, or the movie of a novel the class has read can be shown at the end of term as a reward. On the receiving end are the pupils, most of whom are intimately acquainted with the expressive forms of the new media and knowledgable about the content and implicit references of the youth culture(s), of which they are themselves a part.

Is entertainment educational?

> According to the common notion, there is a very great difference between learning something and having fun. The former may be useful, but only the latter is pleasant. [...]
>
> All we can actually say is that the difference between learning and having fun is not necessarily a natural one, that it has not always been the case and need not continue so for ever. (BRECHT 1963 p. 56; our translation)

This quotation refers to the epic theatre but it is also valid for schools.

Parents and teachers often categorise youth cultures as mere entertainment and not suitable for the classroom. In this sense, entertainment is defined as substandard, non-reflective, non-informative and irrational.

Schools are in a paradoxical situation. On the one hand they are supposed to encourage the pupils' intellectual development: this is their instructional function. On the other hand, they are supposed to teach the pupils how to understand themselves, each other, and the world around them. This is the schools' developmental function. (DROTNER 1991 p. 40).

If the texts of the youth cultures are to be accepted as good educational texts they must build on this paradox. A music video like the above-mentioned "Doggystyle" is chosen by some pupils who identify with the hip hop culture. These pupils introduce their classmates and teacher to their out-of-school interest. In a good teaching situation, these pupils will have the opportunity to tell about their own culture and their favourite music videos, drawing attention to the fact that they have knowledge and competence in an area which is unfamiliar to the others.

When the kids are in the chair and have the chance to verbalise their knowledge, there is a cognitive process which the teacher can work on both verbally and non-verbally. She can also see to it that the other pupils' favourite forms of youth culture are included and confronted with each other. The various pleasures of the various pupils run the show by turns.

In lessons like this the pupils become each other's teachers. In such a situation, the teacher takes the cue from the pupils, though she may choose to be leader of the proceedings and chairperson when the debate speeds up. Her professional knowledge helps her to see what is being underemphasised and who is being left out, and she can interrupt to get the pupils to focus more on neglected areas. She can encourage them to get more information about their own and each other's youth cultures, perhaps by looking at other music videos or by going to the library to borrow magazines. She can interrupt the discussion in order to advance the pupils' visual development, and she can suggest a visit to one or more youth clubs. She can also involve other teachers so that the teaching becomes interdisciplinary.

The Present Moment in a school context

Like most teachers, we are concerned with the possibilities for strengthening the cognitive and affective faculties and integrating them to a greater degree in the teaching process. TV series and music videos thematize irrational sides of the personality which are often unacceptable to teachers in their rational endeavour to qualify the pupils intellectually. Thus the media work on the affective part while the school pulls in the direction of the cognitive part.

In class the pupils will perceive and experience what is going on in many different ways, depending on whether they find it relevant to themselves. The teacher can never know what knowledge will be retained by the individual pupil, and what will be rejected or forgotten. Realization will often come to the pupil in a flash when she or he can relate the content of the teaching to a picture, a scent or a sense of physical unease. When the pupil is grown up the realization will be remembered each time a similar picture or scent is encountered.

In general terms, a person possesses sensory awareness (sight, hearing, smell, feeling and taste), mental thoughts and imaginations, and bodily tensions such as feelings of cold and heat etc. (OLDHAM 1978 pp. 17-18). The body with its senses will function in the present moment, whereas the mind will be oriented towards the past and future. The paradox is that whilst the rational focus of the school is on past events and future possibilities, the body with its senses simply exists in the present moment as invisible energies which advance learning but are not used efficiently to promote development.

The music video is one example of a text which spotlights the present moment and its sensory and bodily processes. It contains elements of the past, the present and the future, as well as fragments of different cultures, and this appeals to many of the pupils. If the teacher dares accept the challenge of this type of media text she will be better able to integrate the affective and cognitive sides of the pupils' personalities.

Invasion and non-acceptance

Some teachers and youth researchers are of the opinion that teaching in and with youth cultures is an improper invasion of the pupils' space. It is seen as a problem that the teacher and the school intrude upon areas where the young construct an identity to liberate them from the adults and their institutions. Another problem is that when this type of teaching takes place in the senior classes it can intrude on feelings which are particularly vulnerable in puberty: by using their senses and bodies the pupils may come into contact with such basic emotions and drives as sorrow, aggression, sexuality and joy (PERLS et al. 1951).

In opposition to this is the fact that school should help the pupils to understand themselves, each other and the society and culture they live in. Seen from this angle, invasion is built into every form of learning, whether aimed at instruction or development.

In a classroom situation, moreover, the pupils are often happy to present and make visible the activities that occupy them in their spare time.

Non-acceptance of the pupils' out-of-school interests, perhaps manifested as a refusal to allow music videos to be used in teaching, would be the antithesis of invasion; it might also impede the pupils' sensory development and body consciousness. We would like to postulate that working with their own youth cultures gives young people the courage to really use their bodies and their senses.

There has to be both invasion and non-acceptance. On the one hand, in accordance with the statement of the aims of the school and with the curriculum of the respective subjects, the teacher has the position of instructor and to some extent of director. Thus a certain degree of invasion is bound to take place. On the other hand, it is up to the pupils themselves to bring in media texts, which means that they contribute to deciding how far youth cultures are accepted as part of the process of education.

It is by working in the force field between invasion and non-acceptance that teachers will best be able to qualify their pupils to be members of a society which needs independent, critical individuals who are able to make their own decisions.

Rudiments of a didactic model

The ideas upon which this article is based can be summed up in a model depicting rotation between 'I' – 'it' – 'we' – 'the world':

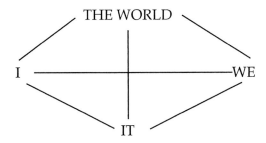

The "I" is the individual pupil or teacher, mind, senses and body. "WE" is the interaction between pupils and teacher(s), and may be regarded as the several groups in the class or as the class as one group. This is where the pupils learn to work together, to speak to each other and to use their senses and their bodies. "IT" is the theme or the text, in this case youth cultures, featuring hip hop, heavy, horses etc. "THE WORLD" is school with its statement of aims, its requirements, its frameworks for social interaction. It is youth cultures and other cultures. It is society with its organisation and ideologies. It is the various demands, existential, psychological, whatever, on the citizens of the future.

In teaching, the aim is to rotate the four areas so that each is foregrounded in turn. If, for example, "IT" is neglected because of a strong orientation towards "I", it is the job of the teacher as director of the lesson to make sure that "IT" comes into the foreground.

Qualifying = quality

In this article we have tried to show that the young people at school today require a new and broader type of qualification involving an extended textuality that integrates verbal and non-verbal expression and regards the multicultural expressive forms of the media as good educational texts.

One characteristic of the new media texts is that they are intertextual. Many music videos contain fragments of narratives, music and symbols which to the untrained viewer may appear chaotic and unconnected though in reality they are references to other music videos, commercials and films – old and new. Thus they contain elements of the past, present and future. They are disjointed and have such a fragmented

131

narrative style that many adults maintain a distance from them.

However, many children and young people are acquainted with the references and show by their body language that they appreciate the innuendos, which are often of a multicultural character. The new media texts transcend national boundaries, both verbally and visually; kids the world over understand the expressive forms of the new youth cultures. But individually they often choose one or more overlapping youth cultures and thus close their minds to the expressive forms of others. Some girls know all about pop and horses, whilst some boys are experts in heavy and techno. Other boys are experts in hip hop and other girls knowledgable about heavy. The class of WEs is a differentiated group of individuals who can tell of a variety of experiences and insights related to their familiarity with the various youth cultures.

Sound, speech, image, light and movement are integrated on the TV screen. This is a form of communication which, appealing as it does to several of the senses, can be defined as **multi-communication**. Looked at quantitatively, **more** is communicated than is normal in teaching by verbal communication. Looked at qualitatively, something **different** is communicated, satisfying the pupils' need for sensory exploration by means of an encounter with cultural models, technology and aesthetics. This encounter may generate realisations which cut across subject, gender, and race, and may even transcend the generational divide if teachers, parents etc. – THE WORLD – are willing to embrace as educational texts the opportunities offered by the youth cultures.

Though we will not go into detail on this point here, it should be emphasised that if such an educational approach is to become a reality it will be necessary to qualify teachers by providing in-service training and suitable teaching material. This will give a more qualified teaching process in general, and will particularly improve the quality of teaching aimed at qualifying the pupils to be members of a society undergoing change and disruption.

Quality teaching can be defined as teaching which qualifies the pupils for the society of the future. It is accepted that the pupils should learn computer skills for this purpose; and it is also important that they develop interdisciplinary skills to cope with the media culture in all its breadth and otherness. In this context, the varied expressive forms of the different youth cultures can provide examples of good educational texts.

Bibliography

BRECHT, B.: *Schriften zum Theater 3. 1933-1947*. Frankfurt am Main, Suhrkamp 1963.

DROTNER, K.: *At skabe sig selv. Ungdom, æstetik, pædagogik*. ("Creating oneself: Youth, aesthetics and educational practice"). Copenhagen, Gyldendal 1991.

OLDHAM, J. et al.: *Risking being alive*. Victoria, Australia; Pit Publishing 1978.

PERLS, F. et al.: *Gestalt Therapy. Excitement and Growth in the Human Personality*. New York, The Julian Press 1951.

ZIEHE, T.: *Ambivalenser og mangfoldighed*. ("Ambivalence and multiplicity"). Copenhagen, Politisk Revy 1989.

The Educational Textmarket: Qualities and Quantities

Torben Weinreich

Despite the fact that a number of new media, principally pictorial media, are increasingly gaining entry into the classroom, even at lower school level, the book is still the most widely used educational medium.[1] According to a cautious estimate, more than three milliard dollars are spent each year in Europe alone on textbooks designed for the first 7-9 years of schooling.

The production of these books is normally regulated with regard to 1) educational legislation, in particular curricular descriptions of the content of individual subjects; 2) dominant trends in educational thought, comprising the interpretation and realization of the legislation made by individual teachers and schools; 3) the economic resources which society makes available for the purchase of teaching material; and 4) the number of pupils.

Book production and social control

Different countries have different traditions regarding the extent to which education, and thus the production of school books, is centrally controlled. At one end of the spectrum we find countries with state publishing houses which completely or largely monopolize the production of the books which the teachers are obliged to use; at the other end, countries with a whole range of privately owned publishing houses producing for a market where it is the individual teacher who selects books for the class, possibly in agreement with the pupils and parents.

Between these extremes there is great national variety. State publishers may exist side by side with privately owned houses, with which they compete, or the state may decree that books may not be used unless they have been approved by a special board, which may or may not be centralized. Finally, the state may control the publication of school books more indirectly, for instance through examination requirements. The degree of control varies from country to country, but no matter how unregulated its selection of teaching material might appear, no country is completely without such control, which often emanates from the wish to maintain a national cultural identity, for instance by ensuring that everyone is acquainted with the classical literature of the nation.

As there is continual change, not only in school legislation, educational trends, the daily routine of the school and the number of pupils, but also in the world which school books reflect and comment on, educational publishers must continually be prepared to renew their stock. They cannot, for expediency's sake, produce an enormous edition of history or geography books and put them in the storeroom in the expectation that they will be able to sell them for the next ten years. On the contrary, the demand for new material and requirements such as new illustrations and different paper quality is more and more frequent in our extremely changeable world. The immediate consequences are that many textbooks, especially for minor school subjects, can only be produced in small editions, which normally means more expensive books.

Fall in production

In many parts in the world, and in fact in almost every European country, the production of school books has decreased within the last two decades, for several reasons:
- Pupil numbers have fallen, simply because the birthrate has dropped, though it appears to be rising again in some countries.
- New and more efficient channels for the distribution of school textbooks have been developed. At the local level, collections of class sets have been established for loan. This means that a school does not need to own so many different books as before but can borrow them from the book-centre as needed.
- With the support of legislation and dominant educational trends, teaching methods have changed, with the result that fewer actual textbooks are used.

- The authorities have made fewer economic resources available to the school system than the decline in pupil numbers can warrant, and it has therefore been necessary to limit spending on books.

It has understandably been difficult for the book trade to continue to insist on the sale of a fixed number of any title in the face of a decline in pupil numbers; similarly, it has had to accept the lower turnover which has resulted from the increased efficiency of distribution. There have certainly been protests about extravagant cuts in funds for teaching materials, but as retrenchments have also been imposed on other social services reduced funding has come to be regarded as an unavoidable if regrettable condition of book production in the country concerned.

What has been most difficult for major sectors of the publishing industry to accept is that changes in educational procedures can result in a less extensive use of school textbooks. And this is actually what has happened in recent years:

- In some subjects, textbooks have been replaced by other books. Instead of a class reading the national literature in special selections designed for particular levels, their teacher may have chosen to use unabridged standard works, and likewise instead of their studying history and geography from specially designed textbooks the teacher may choose to use generally available works dealing with the period or topic which the class is currently working on. Such material will typically be available in class sets from the local book-centre. From the point of view of the publishers, the problem here is not so great: book sales simply move from one section to another.

- Photocopies are used increasingly in schools. Teachers put together their own teaching material from books, journals and newspapers. In Denmark, 800 photocopies per pupil per year are on average handed out in the lower and high schools. A third of this amount is of copyright material. If a typical textbook is approximately 120 pages long, each pupil is given what corresponds to two whole books a year in photocopies largely taken from proper books. This amounts to getting on for a third of the turnover the publishers could have if books were always used instead of photocopies. However, for the schools photocopying is often an expedient, appropriate and cheap way of distributing texts. In many countries a fee is paid per photocopy to the author and the publisher.

- Money is spent on other forms of teaching material, such as films, videos, tapes and computer software. These are often comparatively expensive, especially when the purchase of such permanent apparatus as computers is taken into account.
- The schools are often criticized for being too book-oriented. This criticism comes especially from theorists of creativity and play and from some reformist and liberationist educationalists, including experiential educationalists. These maintain that in biology lessons, for instance, the pupils should not rely on their textbooks but should make investigations out of doors or keep animals and plants in the classroom. It must be emphasized that these educational theories do not in themselves exclude the use of books but reduce or at least change their role.

Denmark: an example

Danish teachers have a large degree of freedom to select teaching materials from a wide variety of publishers. However, every school has a board which in principle has to approve the material chosen, including books, though this rarely gives rise to conflict. Furthermore, teachers may organize their teaching as they wish, in agreement with the pupils and perhaps their parents. It is largely the schools themselves which decide the teaching content and method. There is no state publishing house in Denmark.

In 1993 the Danish parliament passed a new Education Act, which was followed up in 1994-95 with new objectives for the various subjects, a new recommended syllabus and new teaching guides. New subjects, old subjects at new class levels and large changes in other parts of the curriculum necessitate the purchase of among other things new textbooks.

However, neither the state nor the local authorities have given any hope that more funding will be granted. There is, in fact, much to suggest that the book account will be cut as it has been continually since the end of the 70s.

In the period 1980-1993 the number of textbooks sold in Denmark fell by no less than 60%. The general tendency in Europe to a drop in the sale of textbooks was more pronounced in Denmark than in most other countries. The immediate consequence was that fewer titles were issued (a drop of about 20%), and that fewer of each title were sold, resulting in higher prices. The price index for books rose by 120% whilst the general price index rose by 80%. Higher prices meant that schools could afford fewer books, which resulted in smaller editions and further price rises, etc.: a vicious circle.

In 1992, the Danish Publishers' Association and the Writers' Union held a joint conference on "the threatened textbook". A repeated demand from the delegates was that schools should earmark more resources for the purchase of books, preferably so as to regain the level reached at the end of the 70s.

The unexpressed assumption underlying the whole discussion is that schools today are the same as they were in the 70s, which is certainly not the case. The 60% drop in the sale of textbooks has in any case three separate and equally important causes:

- Pupil numbers fell by up to 25% in this period.
- To a higher degree than previously, teachers have elected to use different teaching materials, including books other than textbooks, and frequently to borrow them from collections of class sets.
- Actual budget cuts.

There are strong indications that the picture is much the same in other countries where there has been a decline in the sale of textbooks. The tendency is determined both by market forces and by structural considerations.

And there is one further matter which may have contributed to the falling sales of textbooks: the quality of the books themselves.

The director of a regional centre for teaching materials in Denmark made the following pronouncement shortly after the conference mentioned above:

> The public sector was formerly a good customer, which meant that publishers could risk experimentation, but times have changed. You can't blame them for wanting to survive, but it's a great problem that they are no longer as willing to try out new things as they were before.

Reports produced by Ministry of Education committees since then have criticized the textbooks used in a number of subjects, among them Danish and history.

Textbooks and quality

Textbooks need a variety of qualities. First and foremost they need to present their subject in an educationally effective manner, but they ought also to have aesthetic quality; and both teachers and pupils ought to be able to perceive a quality of usableness. One of these qualities alone is not enough, and neither is high quality in all areas if the textbook is not seen to be the right book at the right time.

It is worth emphasizing that textbooks are rarely used out of the context they were designed for. Children do not usually read textbooks in their spare time: they regard them as books which they are more or less forced to read in or out of school.

This does not mean that the pupils do not demand anything of their textbooks. From the reading they do in their spare time they are acquainted with books whose content and presentation are exciting and interesting. These will to some extent form the pupils' standard for quality in their textbooks; but only to some extent, as children know perfectly well that textbooks are often quite a different matter, and that they (perhaps?) cannot have the same expectations of them.

Because school books are usually designed to be used in specific contexts and with specific age groups, sometimes with a particular class level, both authors and publishers will unavoidably attempt to adapt both the form and content of the books to these specific contexts. The book should be neither more nor less than is exactly required or expected, and this also applies to its quality.

As with most other goods, textbooks can be said to be produced according to the following quality formula:

$$Q = E : A = 1$$
where Q = quality, E = experience and A = anticipation.

The user has certain anticipations which s/he requires the book to live up to. If her/his experience of the book does not live up to these anticipations the quality number will be less than 1. If on the other hand the book exceeds what was anticipated the number will be greater than 1.

No publisher, naturally, will consciously produce books whose quality number is less than 1. Even though experience and anticipation vary from user to user the publisher can still get an impression of the book's success from the sales figures. These are only one among many indications of quality, but a very important one for the publishers, who cannot survive by publishing books which do not sell.

Neither, on the other hand, do the publishers produce books whose quality number is much in excess of 1. They do not send their author on a research trip to South America unless they judge it completely necessary to maintain the quality number at 1. They do not commission the book to be any longer than is necessary, or with illustrations any better than is necessary, and they do not pay the author any more than is necessary. If they did, the price of the book would rise and sales might be smaller as the users would judge it too expensive for their purposes.

The users' anticipations, however, do not appear out of thin air, but to a great extent reflect the knowledge which users, and especially teachers, have of the books which are actually on the market within a subject or topic. The authors and publishers are therefore not only subjected to certain quality requirements but also take part in producing these requirements by virtue of their book production.

Rounding off

The above remarks on the quality of textbooks are valid for a free market with several competing publishers in a situation where teachers have a certain degree of freedom to choose their own teaching material, possibly in consultation with the pupils and their parents. The kind of direct financial support which state publishers usually receive will mean that books can be produced more cheaply, and in such a case the above-mentioned quality formula can to some extent be overlooked; this is especially the case when the state has laid down stringent rules detailing the syllabus for each subject at every level.

I have in the above focused especially on developments in pupil numbers, educational theory and funding which have resulted in a drop in the sale of school textbooks in most European countries in the last two decades. It is important to emphasize that during the same period a number of circumstances might well have led to the level of funding for textbooks being maintained or even increased. New teaching content and lesson forms will create a need not for more books but for new and different ones. So, likewise, will changes in the world outside the classroom, such as the breakup of the Soviet Union and new research findings in subjects taught in the schools.

The problem today is not that schools have too few books: their shelves are groaning with them. It is rather that they are largely the wrong books.

Photo: Kirstine Theilgaard.

Note

1. The statistical information in this article has largely been obtained from the Danish Publishers' Association and Copydan. Other sources are the Danish Book Register and the School Library Year Book.

Selection Mechanisms: Acquiring Teaching Materials for the School Library

Kurt Hartvig Petersen

There is a long-established tradition in Denmark that the pupils' independent investigations and reports are an important element in such subject areas as history, geography, nature studies and social studies. As far as possible the pupils base their work on their own individual lives and interests, so it is consequently important that they seek out the necessary materials by themselves. This means that the material for this kind of teaching must be suitably designed so that pupils can easily and independently acquire the relevant knowledge. It must cover an extremely wide spectrum of topics and fields of interest and yet be simple to read. Therefore it should be organized on library principles.

As in other parts of the world, school libraries in Denmark supply fiction for children and young people to read. But in the last half century they have had the other very important function of acquiring and making available a wide-ranging collection of simple works of non-fiction to be used from time to time in the independent work mentioned above, and otherwise borrowed for out-of-school reading. Media developments have led to the non-fiction collection being expanded with sound tapes, slides, videos, computer programmes and CD-ROM disks of a similar nature.

A catalogue of the teaching material found at present in school libraries in Denmark lists approximately 20,000 non-fiction books and other materials, and 2,000 new titles are published annually. It is quite a job to keep up with the new publications and decide what to acquire from week to week. To help in this, the Danish Library Centre issues a weekly report on all new material for the schools and this is registered centrally.

The ongoing debate

Some of the teaching materials thus registered, the works of fiction and non-fiction which are felt to be most necessary for the libraries to acquire, are described in more detail, giving brief abstracts of their contents, in special news-sheets which are also issued by central bodies. And all audio-visual materials and computer programmes of interest to the schools are described in accounts which focus on their educational function. These descriptions and abstracts, with the evaluations they offer, are used in the weekly meetings in which the school librarians of each municipality discuss the newly issued material and which are followed up by consultations on new acquisitions between librarians and interested teachers in the local schools.

Thus a debate on teaching materials in the school libraries goes on all through the year in the schools and the municipalities. In this debate endeavours are made to examine the teaching materials from the point of view of **the pupils** and to imagine **the possible interaction** between pupil and teaching aid. This approach is thus significantly different from the one that characterizes the writing of most abstracts and reviews of teaching materials, where what is of interest is the actual content and its structure and logic.

Key questions

For the sake of clarity, the most important points in the current debate on teaching materials will here be tabulated in the practical form of **a set of questions**. This is used in the training of school librarians at The Royal Danish School of Educational Studies:

Purpose and content

- Will the material train the pupil in the subject's skills, working methods or forms of expression?
- Will it give exact information or confront the pupil with human destinies, courses of events, environments or conflicts?
- Will it discuss particular questions with the pupil?
- Will it convince the pupil that certain views, ideas or values are correct?

Narrative form

- Do the language and text / illustrations / screen graphics / visuals / sound track give the pupils clear and graphic ideas about relations and events within the subject?
- Will the pupils make their own observations from the pictures, or is there any other kind of appeal to their curiosity?
- Are the pupils helped by a clear and simple summary or user interface?
- If necessary, are the pupils able to select supplementary descriptions and pick freely from the text?
- Are complex general matters illustrated by "good examples" which the pupils can relate to?
- Are the pupils presented with good human stories?
- Will the pupils react emotionally to contrasts, provocations, the unexpected, the different, violence and injustice?
- Will the material provide an experience of direct interaction with reality via simulations, use of database, extramural activities or other means?

Activities

- Do the suggestions for activities lead the pupils to follow instructions or find out information?
- Are the pupils led to discover the appropriate procedure?
- Are the pupils led to investigate, experiment, make discoveries and explain regularities?
- Are the pupils led to summarize and describe a given topic?
- Are the pupils led to reflect, discover new questions, gather further information, make further observations and construct their own explanations?
- Are the pupils led to produce reports?
- Are the pupils led to express their own experiences?
- Does the material get the pupils to perceive and formulate views and values?
- Does it encourage the pupils to debate, take positions and use their initiative?

Comments on the questions

The following presents a brief commentary on the background to this set of questions.

It can be asserted that the questions concerning narrative form are the most important. The pupils' independent work stands or falls on the clarity of the material referred to, and it is important that it quickly catches their attention.

Very many books and other teaching aids assume that in a given situation the pupils may need to draw up an account of a topic and that the information they give will be useful. One can often detect an author's assumption that children are able to learn a stream of facts if only they are presented clearly, logically and in short sentences. In many cases the exposition is reminiscent of a textbook's, and can be said to lack epic strength.

It may seem natural to choose the expository form of a textbook for the numerous books designed to give information on exact, objective, non-controversial subjects such as hydroelectric power, social insects or medieval buildings. But then it will be extremely important to use language which connects with the pupils' preconceptions and gives them definite images on their "inner screens". Dramatic or richly detailed illustrations will also be needed to arouse the pupils' curiosity, and a deliberate lexivisual correlation between text and illustration will also be important.

Similar observations on language and on the correlation of visuals and sound-track apply to videos and other audiovisual aids.

Many computer programmes also aim simply at communicating information on some subject area. The graphics in such programmes must be used to their maximum, and the user interface must naturally be easy for the pupils to manage. In this context, computer programmes using the hypertext principle are of interest. Here the pupil can move freely around the whole textual area. With hypertext it is necessary to be aware of the possibilities for "clicking" into further explanations and descriptions if they are discovered to be necessary. These may take the shape of text, sound, or either still and moving pictures.

Media and narrative form

The book, the sound medium and the video are narrative media, so it is well worth considering what types of material can be transmitted as narrative. It will be advantageous to choose the narrative form rather than an impersonal theoretical form if the intention is to confront the pupils with human destinies, foreign environments or conflicts past or present. The narrative form can be the correct choice when it is important that the pupils are made to experience the topic personally and to formulate their own questions as the basis for further reading and the drawing up of reports. And the narrative form will similarly be the obvious choice when it is advantageous to illuminate a complex situation such as a political conflict with one or more "good examples", such as powerful narratives concerning people caught up in the conflict whose fate reflects its nature and possible causes.

A more progressive narrative form like this will to some extent make use of novelistic strategies. A documentary account or faction, the deliberate mixture of fact and fiction, may be used. The narrative will always have a central character whom the pupils can relate to, and it will often aim at surprise or shock.

In most cases it is clear that a progressive narrative form is indissolubly connected with a wish to illuminate a viewpoint or get the pupils to endorse it, or that the teaching aid regards particular ethical or moral values as right. Such intentions are often not obvious before one has looked at the directions for activities. In many cases, of course, the suggested topics for discussion give the pupils genuine opportunities for an independent consideration of views and adoption of values, but the formulations used in the text and inductions to the discussions may reveal an attempt to convert the pupils to a particular point of view.

A book giving a great deal of information about medieval castles. The illustrations are extremely informative, and the pupils have every opportunity of basing their own observations and their own narratives on them. F. Macdonald and M. Bergin: A medieval castle. The Salariya Book Co. Ltd., 1990.

Simulations

Traditional teaching aids describe reality, some more intensely than others. In recent years, teaching aids have appeared which try to give a more direct experience of actually being in a fragment of reality. Simulation games are a 25-year-old phenomenon. In a simulation the pupils finds themselves in a fictional world, a strictly limited piece of reality. They are restricted to the actions predetermined by the constructor of the game.

The best simulations put their players in situations where they must find out for themselves where the problem lies. The procedures of a town council, or the options of a voluntary worker revealing some Third World problems are typical cases.

PCs have increased the possibilities for constructing simulations whose fictional environments and societies are so detailed that they are very convincing; and the computer can very quickly show players the consequences of the decisions they make in the course of the game. And the best simulations force pupils to express themselves precisely about their experiences in the fictional world of the game, and to think about their connection with reality.

Databases and "explorations"

It can be claimed that the raw data in databases are a good bit closer to reality, even though here too there has of course been a certain amount of filtering and adaptation. If the user interface is easily managed by the pupils, on-line and CD-ROM bases will give them a chance to make use of such a range of data when investigating problems that they can get to connect data which in principle have never been connected before. The best results can be quite original. It is completely different from working with a textbook whose author has adapted and predigested the topic for the pupil.

A faction book about the Israeli-Palestinian conflict. Two fictional characters, an Israeli soldier and a stone-throwing Palestinian boy, are central figures. The Israeli soldier is a "dove" who makes fruitless attempts to prevent his comrades from committing outrages. A strong narrative with a clear viewpoint: the Israelis are oppressors and the Palestinians have a right to their own land. Photo: Polfoto.

In conclusion, it is necessary to be very careful with the kind of teaching aid which offers suggestions for activities that send the pupil out to explore the real world. When, for example, pupils go out to interview the mayor they will hardly be told anything he hasn't said before; but they may still have the experience of being real journalists nosing out new statements. But can the teaching aid provoke the pupils to formulate questions which beget new questions in a proper conversation on matters having to do with the pupils' actual situation?

When a teaching aid gets pupils to investigate the water plants in a marsh there are hardly going to be any epoch-making scientific findings, but the pupils may well feel a personal concern for the results of their observations. It is extremely important to see whether the activities suggested by the teaching aid really stimulate the pupils to experiment, find their own interpretations and communicate them, or whether the pupils simply follow instructions and confirm what the author has previously related.

Textbooks too

This account has focused on the background to the choice of educational aids for the school library, i.e. material that is designed to be suitable for self-learning.

There are quite a few textbook systems and related materials which are meant to be worked through by the pupils with the help of their teacher. These are mainly designed for structured teaching which aims to give the pupils exact knowledge and instruction in the mother tongue and foreign languages, and in mathematics and science in the senior classes. The choice of such materials will depend on whether they are related to the subject content and working methods described in the curriculum. A rough estimate is also made of the book's linguistic and conceptual level and its external appearance. But no set of generally accepted criteria has been developed for such teaching materials, and there are no arrangements for organizing their ongoing examination, discussion and acquisition. The pupils have no influence on the selection of such materials, which are simply handed out to them.

In conclusion, it should be added that there is a growing tendency in Denmark for school libraries to include teaching materials of the textbook type in their collections. More and more schools are finding this practical. This means that in future textbook material will also be included in the ongoing debate on teaching aids administered by school libraries. One consequence could be that materials designed for structured teaching with the teacher in control of textbook dominated subjects could be replaced by teaching aids conducive to pupil-centred, pupil-controlled independent work.

Research on Pedagogic Texts:
An Approach to the Institutionally and Individually Constructed Landscapes of Meaning

Staffan Selander

The aim of this article is to outline some perspectives on research on "pedagogic texts" or, to use the more proper English term, "educational media".[1] With "pedagogic texts/educational media" we shall mean not only school textbooks but the whole range of possible texts + pictorial illustrations + films + computer programmes which are produced for educational purposes, i.e. to inform and convince the reader, viewer or listener that the information and perspectives presented are true and correct. This kind of information will be defined as institutionally framed manifestations.[2] The producer is an authority like "The School", "The Labour Market", "The Television News" or "The Health Care System", and the texts are information or instructions in articles, textbooks, pamphlets, brochures, videos, reports etc. The reader is not any reader, but one who is role-defined: a pupil, a student, a client, a patient, a citizen etc. To understand a pedagogic text does not only imply understanding its content: more importantly, it means understanding its social function and its relations to "institutional common sense" and the stratification of power in society. (Cf. the overall model on page 172 ff. below).

In the first part of this article, research on **school textbooks** will be highlighted. The second part will focus on important **theoretical and textual aspects** of the 'pedagogic text', and the third on a **system-oriented approach** towards the understanding of educational media. In the final part conclusions will be drawn for **future research** on non-fiction in the school context, especially on a broad understanding of pedagogic texts and new media in education.

---

1. It is difficult to translate the Swedish term "pedagogik", because it is neither 'pedagogy' nor 'education', even though the latter, broader term is closer than the former.
2. SELANDER 1993 p. 75 discusses "institutional manifestation" in relation to the Durkheimian concept 'collective representation'.

Lines of research

What does it mean to interpret a 'text'? Traditionally, different answers have been given. We can focus on the 'author' and aspects related to personality, biography or culture. In that case we will be interested in questions related to the writer's intentions or options to personal or cultural meanings. We can also focus on the text itself, on its content or its linguistic construction. We can focus on the 'reader' and the reception of the text, examining its personal or cultural meaning. Or we may be interested in questions related to the textmarkets and to the marketing of texts – in texts as economic artifacts. And we may have a specific interest in the development of texts and illustrations, from handwritten books to modern typography.

Today there seems to be a general agreement that the author has no exclusive rights to the interpretation of the text. New meanings emerge in new contexts. The written product becomes detached from the author and acquires its own life in relation to new contexts and the aspirations and needs of others. Any reader can take any text and make his or her reading of it, at least as far as fiction is concerned. Thus, to understand a text (in a general sense) is to understand it in relation to one's own individual purpose, needs, experience, knowledge and interests. However, to understand a text also means to understand it in relation to a cultural, social and historical situation or process.[3] In the following we will focus on the specific meaning of nonfiction in the school context.

Research on the meaning and social significance of texts is of course no new enterprise. "The Great Texts" like the Bible, texts in philosophy, jurisprudence and literary texts have especially been the focus of scholarly investigation from the 18th century (Schleiermacher) to postmodern deconstructivism (Derrida). Other researchers have been interested in "utility texts", such as political pamphlets[4], journalism[5], technical information[6], popular science[7] or nonfiction for children[8]. For the latter, semiotics, rhetoric, theory of style and discourse analysis have been

3. SELANDER 1984 pp. 3 ff.
4. TULLY 1988.
5. HULTÉN et al. 1988.
6. MÅRDSJÖ 1992.
7. GUNNARSSON 1987.
8. GOMEZ 1991.

Illustration from the book "De skapande varelsernas sedelärande samtal", 1483. This book was probably the first pedagogic text printed in Sweden, the topic being the world and how one should relate to it, i.e. knowledge and moral. The Royal Library, Stockholm.

the principal theoretical perspectives, whilst in the study of "The Great Texts" hermeneutics and deconstructivism have also been used. Additional perspectives have been taken into consideration in research on school textbooks: textbook production, the school as a system, the nature of university disciplines or specific school subjects, how pupil learn and research on reading skills. In the following, Scandinavian research will be especially discussed. A worldwide overview will be found in JOHNSEN 1993.

The school as a system provides the perspective in the "frame factor theory" developed by Urban Dahllöf and used in studies of teachers' choices of textbooks and of textbooks as a resource in the interplay between different factors such as time, place, group size etc.[9] Only a few studies exist of textbooks at university level; there is, for instance, a philosophically oriented study of university textbooks on statistics[10]. School subjects such as history, physics, religion etc. have been the basis for many didactically oriented approaches.[11] The emergence of school subjects has been studied from the perspective of power relations in society[12] or using a teacher–constructivist approach.[13]

Relations between textbooks and learning, or "non-learning", have been highlighted, and an increasing interest in phenomenological studies on pupils' learning styles is noticeable.[14] Research on how children read is of interest to both educational researchers and linguists.[15] Another line of research has been directed towards the production of textbooks[16], and another still on the content aspects, especially "ideologi-kritik", or the critical understanding of ideological biases.[17] Research based on rhetoric and on discursive and concept-oriented perspectives also constitutes an expanding field of research.[18]

The discursive regulation of mind

As an example of a 'pedagogic text', let us take the textbook – a traditional text produced for educational purposes. This text is "fan-sha-

9. BROMSJÖ 1965 p. 7; DAHLLÖF et al. 1971 pp. 11-15, 135 f.; LUNDGREN et al. 1982. Other related aspects can be found in *SOU 1971:91*; AXELSSON & ODIN 1982; WESTBURY 1982; ELLIOT & WOODWARD 1990 pp. 127 ff.; JUHLIN 1994 p. 3; GAREFALAKIS 1994 pp. 20 ff.
10. MOLANDER 1987.
11. ANDOLF 1972; OLSSON 1986; KARLSSON 1987; LÖFDAHL 1987; HÄRENSTAM 1993.
12. POPKEWITZ (ed.) 1987 pp. 10 ff.
13. GOODSON 1988.
14. ENGESTRÖM 1990; STABERG 1992; AHLBERG 1992.
15. JOHANSEN 1991; HENE et al. 1991.
16. APPLE et al. 1991.
17. KORITZINSKY 1977; HAAVELSRUD 1979; NORDKVELLE 1987; FRITZSCHE 1991.
18. SELANDER 1984, 1988; de CASTELL et al. 1989; SELANDER et al. (eds.) 1994.

ped" or organized in "facets", different units built on the same basic structural principle. This **facet structure** seems to be related to the demands of the written curriculum and to the 40-45 minutes time schedule in schools.[19]

The **rhetorical register** in the texts is related to its persuasive and convincing character, the strategies it uses to convince the reader that the information given is true, reliable, useful and important. The rhetorical register can be internal or external, depending on the context. "Internal" refers to the text itself, its persuasive character; "external" to the fact that the text is embedded in a structure where one person, i.e. the teacher, has the authority to determine what is important. The television news reporter has a similar function of giving the "contextual clues" to the fragments of information, the flow of non-interrelated pieces.

At present interest in the rhetorical register is noticeably increasing.[20] The rhetorical tradition is derived from speech acts in the senate and the court and from panegyrics on great leaders in ancient Greece and Rome.[21] During the 18th century its conventions were criticised both by scientists and by the romantic poets: they stated that writing and printing should not be overloaded and that the text should contain correct statements concerning nature or, in literary texts, be related to personal feelings. In spite of this, the ubiquity of rhetoric nowadays has been remarked upon. The renewed interest in rhetoric in contemporary society seems to be related to the expansion of the radio- and TV-media, the daily newspapers, advertisements, pictorial illustrations and films.

Logos, ethos and pathos are the three pillars of the rhetorical tradition. *Logos* refers to the facts and the arguments; *ethos* to the speaker's credibility and whole personality; and *pathos* to different ways of getting the audience interested and emotionally involved. All three aspects are used today in the modern mass media as well as in scientific publications, and sometimes even in school textbooks.[22] To under-

19. SELANDER 1988 p. 30.
20. Examples of classical rhetoric can be read in Demosthenes, Cicero and Lysias. Introductions to the field will be found in FAFNER 1982; LINDHARDT 1987; VICKERS 1988; and JOHANNESSON 1990. Rhetoric in new fields can be found in SKYUM-NIELSEN 1992; ROKSVOLD 1991; and PRELLI 1989.
21. NYSTRÖM 1994.
22. In school textbooks, *pathos* was formerly prevalent in the text itself, but nowadays has moved to the pictorial illustrations. Thus it is important to analyze both the textual character and the pictorial character of the textbook.

stand the rhetorical character of pedagogic texts/educational media will be an important part of the analysis of how the texts/pictures operate to inform and convince the reader.

Another register is **instruction and control**. In the pedagogic text the reader is often instructed, i.e. he or she is told to do certain things in relation to a text which is often formulated at the end of the chapters as questions and exercises. The author rarely starts with a question or a problem and then develops the text in relation to this. We will show two different examples of the author's/textbook's relation to the material presented and the way questions can be asked:[23]

> How can we know anything about the way people lived a hundred thousand years ago? Some of it we can guess, most of it we know nothing about. Although these people lived such a long time ago, historians can say some things about their lives with a reasonable degree of certainty [...] *Sources.* For the oldest history the most important sources are those that archaeologists find during excavations. [...] Another way of acquiring knowledge about how people lived in prehistoric times is to study peoples who still live as hunters and collectors. [...]
> 1. Which were the first human beings? When, approximately, did they live?
> 2. When did the human species to which we belong appear?
> 3. What did the first human beings live on? [...]
> 10. How can we know anything about how people lived during prehistoric times?

In another textbook the same problems are dealt with differently:[24]

> Scientists and historians are rather like detectives. If they do not know the answer to a problem or mystery, they gather as much evidence as they can to help them find a solution. [...]
> Detective's report [...] Mystery [...] Case [...] Experiment [...] Evidence [...]
> Consider your verdict.
> Check the facts.
> Think for yourself.
> Be a detective.

In the first example the text seems congruent with the older conventions of text–reading practice, where an interpreter knows the correct answers. In the second case the text is treated as a tool for reflective understanding and gives an opportunity for research-like activities. Both texts were produced for 15-year-old pupils.

23. ÖHMAN 1989 pp. 10 ff. (Our translation).
24. COUPE & ANDREWS 1984 pp. 7 ff.

Textual styles

Textual styles in pedagogic texts refer to different modalities; thus there are ostensive, narrative or discursive styles. The **ostensive** text points at the world and says: "Look here, this is called ...". This is the most prevalent text-type, as in the following:[25]

> Many important inventions came from Mesopotamia. [...] metals instead of stone for weapons and tools. As early as 6000 B.C. they started to use copper. [...] It was not until 1000 B.C. that people learned how to make steel out of iron. [...] Other important inventions were the plough and the wheel. [...] Sumerian priests also made a calendar, the oldest one in history. To do this, they had to study the movements of celestial bodies. [...] Astronomy [...] is a science which originated in Sumeria 5000 years ago.

The idea might be to give the pupils 'concepts' with which to understand the world, but too often the books only teach new words without relating them to concepts or to ways of organizing knowledge. An "objectivist bias" is frequently apparent: the text assumes that the word correctly mirrors the world (nature, society etc.), that the signifier is the same as the signified. "Experiental realism" – the philosophical acceptance of both the "reality of the world" and the psychological and social constraints in our construction of concepts to understand this world – is not in evidence. And finally, it seems that concepts are not consciously chosen at a "prototype" level from which a deeper understanding (both in terms of generalizations and of sub-categories) might emerge.[26] The prototype level is the one we identify in everyday life. We normally use 'table', for example, as an identifying concept, which on the one hand can be generalized to 'furniture', on the other hand specified to 'kitchen table', 'bedroom table' etc.

The **narrative** text tells us a story with a plot. This kind of text has formerly been used in history textbooks, for example, relating tales about kings and queens, heroes and villains. It is often "archetypal", like the basic structure of fairy-tales or TV soap operas: there are numerous examples of representatives sent out to save the nation or of a common sacrifice for the same purpose:[27]

25. ÖHMAN 1989 p. 14. (Our translation).
26. LAKOFF 1987 pp. 58 ff.
27. ODHNER & WESTMAN 1930 part II p. 11. (Our translation).

Now Gustav Adolf equipped the army and navy to take part in the great war in Germany. Before he sailed he summoned his parliament and took a warm farewell of his councillors. "God is my witness", he said, "that I do not embark on this war without cause, or from love of battle, but I have been constrained to it because the emperor has given succour to our Polish enemies. The oppressed Protestants have also implored my help to liberate them from the Papal yoke."

The narrative modality dominated before WW2, at least in the Nordic countries. Today a new interest is shown in writing "stories", and this is sometimes discussed as a solution for modern textbooks.

Our present preoccupations seem to be the ones that define how we understand – and how we write – history.[28] The concepts used in history-writing will only occasionally be explained. Pupils are not usually given the basic tools to understand history or society. Concepts such as 'the nation', which arose relatively recently, may be used to explain events, wars, conflicts etc. which took place long before the 19th century.

The **discursive** text is constructed by means of arguments designed to deepen the readers' understanding of a phenomenon. It does not only teach the names of things, or tell a good story,[29] but highlights a "problem" or a "question", presents arguments, adduces examples and counter-examples, discusses facts, and displays "patterns" or "explanations". The idea behind this modality is not to prescribe an understanding of "x", but to invite the reader to take part in the construction of the phenomenon:[30]

A minority is a national group with a common heritage of race, language, religion and nationality, which is separated from the politically dominant cultural group. [...] This definition underlines the fact that minorities are in a dangerous position. They are afraid of discrimination (like the negroes in the United States, the Jews in many countries during different periods of time) or regimentation (e.g. Poles or Finns during the times of russification in Russian history). [...] The problematique of a minority group is also influenced by geographical factors [...] 'minorities in blocks' (minorities which are concentrated in a particular area) [...] and 'spread–out minorities'. [...] Another line of demarcation is also important here: there are cooperative minorities (e.g. Swedish–speaking people in Finland) and hostile ones (e.g. one part of the population in Alsace in relation to Germany 1871–1919).

28. See van LEEUWEN & SELANDER 1995.
29. SVENSSON 1995.
30. BROLIN et al. 1968 p. 100. (Our translation.)

The social regulation of mind

'Understanding' a text may be taken to mean that the reader "is not puzzled". Let us take the following example: On the lawn there is a sign saying "Keep off the grass!" What does it mean to understand this text? If someone reads it and does not (consciously) put his foot on the grass, does that mean that he understands the text? And consider the following possibility: someone reads the text **and** steps onto the grass in protest against "the rules of society". Is this also an example of "understanding the text"?[31] Most of us would agree that it is. Well, now think of the following context: the textbook and the teacher give some specific information. A pupil who knows how to repeat this information in tests is seen as someone who understands the topic. Still it is quite possible that though he repeats the sentences correctly he **is** still puzzled. However, the school would (in most cases) consider a correct answer as demonstrating understanding (knowledge) rather than achievement, which is perhaps the more proper name for it.

Every text, fiction or non-fiction, has an "implied reader" (or readers) whom the author has in mind and is addressing.[32] School textbooks, for example, are written for different, psychologically defined, stages of age (the heritage from Piaget). Sometimes we find books written specifically for girls or boys. An important point is that non-fiction is also often produced for a specific reader: a client, a patient, a pupil etc. And in the school context where the reading is tested by the teacher, the pupil is an "actual reader". It is not given that a text produced for a school stage and an abstractly defined reader will suit every actual reader. When problems occur, teachers usually try to adapt the actual reader to the text, and if that does not succeed, the pupil is given a textbook produced for an earlier stage or class.

This indicates some important aspects of 'pedagogic texts': they cannot be understood in the same way as other texts. Pedagogic texts are "closed", not "open"; they are institutionally defined and (most often) used in a context where we (traditionally) have one person who knows the correct answer (the teacher) and others (the pupils) who are checked up on and tested in relation to the correct answer. When Umberto Eco writes about the "reader", he does not mean this kind of

31. HERRMANN 1992 p. 7.
32. LUNDSTEN 1992.

institutionally defined reader.[33] A **system-oriented** and **historical** understanding of the pedagogic text is needed. An overview of the history of pedagogic texts will give the following (broad) picture:

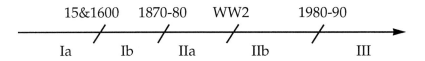

Figure 1. A historical overview of texts in education.

Period Ia starts in ancient Greece and period Ib with the rise of printing technology and the first school textbooks (by Ramus and Comenius respectively). However, throughout this period (I) the spoken word is of primary importance, and the textbooks used are mostly novels, grammars, mathematics and the catechism. Learning by heart is essential, and rhetoric is an important tool.

During period IIa mass education is organized. School textbooks are produced for regular use in classrooms, and listening gives way to reading and writing activities. During period IIb textbooks are characterized by new printing techniques, pictorial illustrations and later on by whole packages of preproduced teaching materials. Throughout this period (II) teachers control content and textual practices in the classrooms.

During period III mass media and computer technology are increasingly used in the classroom. Gradually control moves from the teacher to the learner. A new role for the teacher emerges: no longer a "street level bureaucrat", she or he becomes a tutor or guide for the learners, who now seek information from many different sources over which the teacher has no control.

These snapshots give some clues to the historical role of the school textbook. Educational media of different kinds will be used, including new media which were not originally produced for educational purposes. These historical shifts will also influence the relations between authors, texts and readers. The first shift is from fiction to non-fiction textbooks in schools.

33. ECO 1987.

Literature	Textbook
Author	School + teacher
Text	Text
Reader	Student
Hermeneutic spiral	Pedagogic spiral

Figure 2. Differences between text as literature and text as school textbook.

Our first distinction will be between **fiction** and **non-fiction**. The former deals with a fantasy world whilst the latter deals with a real world; the former cannot be corrected relative to facts, the latter can. However, rhetoric (metaphors, metonymies etc.) is used in both.

The second distinction will be between the text and **the interested reader** on the one hand, and the text and its controlled use in **a school context** on the other. In the latter case the identity of the author seems to be of little interest: the context is more important, and the reader is defined as a student or a pupil.

The reading of the text will be our third distinction. The reader of literature will use what is called "a **hermeneutic circle** or spiral": to understand the whole he needs to understand the parts; but as soon he has a good grasp of the whole, he will understand the parts in a new way. The reading of the text in the school is different: the **pedagogic spiral**[34] starts with the teacher, who may tell about, for instance, pages 47 to 54. The pupils will then read these pages for homework, and the day after the teacher will test their achievement, but not necessarily their understanding.

The use of textbooks in schools includes **norm-activating** processes: on the one hand socially defined values (individual v. collective ideals; democratic v. communistic ideals; patriarchal v. feminist perspectives etc.), on the other hand socially defined aspects of knowledge and of what counts as knowledge (to be able to specify and name things; to be able to solve problems; to be able to make things work out in practice etc.).[35] The pedagogic text also presupposes a "priest", a **person who functions as controller**, defining the meaning and testing the readers' understanding and achievement in reading the text.

34. SELANDER 1988 p. 21.
35. MOLANDER 1987 pp. 24 ff.

However, IT (Information Technology) is now effecting a huge transformation of information structures and links in society which will probably change the relation between text and reader in the school context. The boundaries of fiction and non-fiction are blurred when new media enter schools.

Textbook	New media in education
School + teacher	School + instructor/tutor
Text	IT and other media
Student	Student
Pedagogic spiral	IPA – Information Processing Activities

Figure 3. Traditional pedagogic spiral in relation to IT and IPA (Information Processing Activities).

It is possible that the new media in schools and new information processing activities will lead to new text-reading practices which are more like the traditional relation between literature and reader: open-ended rather than closed, interest-based rather than predefined and thematically oriented rather than facet-structured. If information is floating around in the computer networks (the Internet etc.), and if pupils and students are allowed to seek information, the role of the teacher will change from administrator of a predefined text to a tutor who provides the structure and instruments to evaluate and seek information from the huge quantity available. However, the extent to which this is realised will depend on the emerging power relations in society.

It is, as has been argued, important to "frame" the pedagogic text, whilst doing one's best to avoid falling into the cave of structuralism. When van Dijk talks about frames, he indicates[36] an

ORGANIZATIONAL PRINCIPLE, relating a number of concepts which by CONVENTION and EXPERIENCE somehow form a 'unit' which may be actualized in various cognitive tasks, such as language production and

36. van DIJK 1977 pp. 159 ff. There seems to be a great advantage in using 'frame' instead of 'code', which has so many connotations that it has lost its meanings. See e.g. ECO 1984 pp. 164 ff. In educational research, the term has denoted "social codes" (Bernstein), "curriculum codes" (Lundgren) and "school codes" (Arfwedson). KRESS 1993 p. 187 argues that 'context' is also too vague a concept and could be replaced by 'interrelated semiotic systems'.

comprehension, perception, action and problem solving [...]. The point of introducing frames into model structures is that the interpretation of sentences would no longer be relative only to the sequence of previous sentences of a discourse, but also relative to the set of propositions of a particular frame.

Scholes argues that even though constraints are necessary to understanding, we should not forget the constructivist character of the reading of a text:[37]

> The existence of specific discursive codes seems to me beyond argument, and their constraining effect on the actual practice of writing is a necessary corollary of their existence; but it would be unwarranted to assume from this that such constraints are absolute and fixed. Codes change. Discursive practice modifies discursive systems, which are never completely closed. In short, there is always room for creativity in any discursive order, but it is attained by mastering the practice of the discourse to a degree that enables new utterances to be formed, which in turn become a part of the body of discursive models, and finally effect changes in the code itself.

Perspectives for future research

Traditional pedagogic texts have been framed by the institutionalised "school" for which they are produced, since WW2 largely by professionals working within that institution. However, the media used in contemporary schools are not primarily produced for this context, and thus it is of great importance to take note of the process by which these new media and their related genres are **adapted to** the "school", and the use which is made of them in this context.

A related aspect is the pragmatic study of how pedagogic texts / educational media are used in classroom settings – not only in terms of "How often they are used" but rather in terms of "Which parts are used?" and "In which ways are they used?" It will be of interest to study the social construction of meaning and understanding, related to the role of the texts, pictorial illustrations, films and databases. Therefore a shift in research emphasis seems to be needed, from a theory-driven approach where hypotheses are tested, to **a problem-driven approach** where the focus will be on the questions and problems encountered by teachers and students, how they try to solve their prob-

37. SCHOLES 1985 p. 144.

lems and the role of new educational media in this respect. A problem-driven approach will also embrace areas related to organizational framing, social interaction and mental processes: i.e., organizational, sociological, psychological, economic, linguistic and discursive perspectives.[38] And, as Posner et al. have argued, if learning is to be rationally based:[39]

> [...] the students will need to be immunized against the kind of inevitable indoctrination that occurs when neither teacher nor student is aware of his own fundamental assumptions [...] Sufficient observational theory should be taught.

This approach also points to the interesting possibilities of developing speech act theories and perspectives related to activities like reading and telling, doing and using. Thus there can be interest in both contextual aspects (frames, codes etc.) and aspects related to the dynamics of individual construction of meanings from texts, in the widest sense of the term.

A third aspect seems to be the development and production of **discursive textual styles** for educational use. When information is floating around in different systems it will be more and more important for the individual to be able to select it with discrimination in order to produce knowledge. From a democratic point of view, too, the production of "good and relevant" knowledge will require this.

Bibliography

AHLBERG, A.: *Att möta matematiska problem. En belysning av barns lärande*. Gothenborg, University of Gothenburg 1992.

ANDOLF, G.: *Historien på gymnasiet. Undervisning och läroböcker 1820-1965*. Stockholm, Esselte Studium 1972.

APPLE, M. & L.K. CHRISTIAN-SMITH: *The Politics of the Textbook*. New York, Routledge 1991.

AXELSSON, V. & B. ODIN: *Läromedelsresurser och deras användning. En studie av två kommuners hantering av läromedelsfrågorna för grundskolan*. Uppsala, University of Uppsala 1982.

38. EVENSEN 1986 p. 18.
39. POSNER et al. 1982 pp. 224 ff.

BROMSJÖ, B.: *Samhällskunskap som skolämne. Målsättningar, kursinnehåll och arbetssätt på den grundläggande skolans högstadium.* Stockholm, Svenska Bokförlaget Norstedts-Bonniers 1965.

BROLIN, P.E. et al.: *Historiens huvudlinjer. Tematiska återblickar. Åk 2–3.* Stockholm, Almqvist & Wiksell 1968.

de CASTELL, S. et al.: *Language, Authority and Criticism. Readings on the School Textbook.* London, The Falmer Press 1989.

COUPE, S. & M. ANDREWS: *Their Ghosts May Be Heard – Australia to 1900.* Melbourne, Longman Cheshire 1984.

DAHLLÖF, U. & E. WALLIN: *Läromedelsforskning och undervisningsplanering.* Lund, Studentlitteratur 1971.

Demosthenes, Cicero. Tre politiska tal. (Bertil Cavallin). Stockholm, Forum pocket 1973.

van DIJK, T.A.: *Text and Context. Explorations in the Semantics and Pragmatics of Discourse.* London and New York, Longman 1977.

ECO, U.: *Semiotics and the Philosophy of Language.* London, Macmillan Press 1984.

ECO, U.: *The Role of the Reader. Explorations in the Semiotics of Texts.* London, Hutchinson 1987.

ELLIOT, D.L. & A. WOODWARD: *Textbooks and Schooling in the United States.* (= NSSE Yearbook). Chicago, The University of Chicago Press 1990.

ENGESTRÖM, Y.: *Learning, Working and Imagining. Twelve Studies in Activity Theory.* Helsinki, Orienta-Konsultit 1990.

EVENSEN, L.S.: A note on the relationship between theory and application. In: EVENSEN, L.S. (ed.): *Nordic Research in Text Linguistics and Discourse Analysis.* Trondheim, Tapir 1986.

FAFNER, J.: *Tanke og tale.* Copenhagen, C.A. Reitzel 1982.

FRITZSCHE, P.: Xenophobia and Prejudice – a Problem for Human Rights Education. Paper presented at the 14th Scientific Meeting of the ISPP, University of Helsinki, July 1–5, 1991.

GAREFALAKIS, J.: *Läroboken som traditionsbärare. Om hemspråksundervisningen i grekiska. Ett läroplansteoretiskt och didaktiskt perspektiv.* Stockholm, HLS 1994.

GOMEZ, E.: Faktaboken – en bortglömd genre inom barnlitteraturen. In: *SPOV. Studier av den pedagogiska väven 12*, 1991, pp. 11-23.

GOODSON, I.: *The Making of Curriculum: Collected Esays.* London, Falmer 1988.

GUNNARSSON, B.–L. (ed.): *Facktext.* Malmö, Språkvårdssamfundets skrifter 1987.

HAAVELSRUD, M.: *Indoktrinering eller politisering? Form og innhold i ungdomsskolens undervisning i samfunnskunskap.* Oslo, Universitetsforlaget 1979.

HENE, B. & S. WAHLÉN: Barns läsutveckling och läsning. In: *Rapport från ASLA:s höstsymposium Stockholm 15-16 november 1990.* Uppsala universitet, FUMS 1991.

HERRMANN, E.: *Om tolkning. II. Att förstå.* Uppsala, Svenska kyrkans forskningsråd 1992.

HULTÉN, B. et al.: *Journalister. Invandrare. Flyktingar.* Stockholm, Journalisthögskolan 1988.

HÄRENSTAM, K.: *Skolboks-islam. Analys av bilden av islam i läroböcker i religionskunskap.* Gothenburg, University of Gothenburg 1993.

JOHANNESSON, K.: *Retorik eller konsten att övertyga.* Stockholm, Norstedts 1990.

JOHANSEN, J. (ed.): *Debat om læseudvikling – en artikelsamling.* Copenhagen, Danmarks Pædagogiske Institut 1991.

JOHNSEN, E.B.: *Textbooks in the Kaleidoscope. A Critical Survey of Literature and Research on Educational Texts.* Oslo, Scandinavian University Press 1993.

JUHLIN, A.-C.: *Läromedelsval och läromedelsstöd i gymnasieskolan.* Uppsala, University of Uppsala 1994.

JULKUNEN, M.-L. et al.: *Research on Texts at School.* Joensuu, Joensuu University 1991.

KARLSSON, K.-G.: *Historieundervisning i klassisk ram. En didaktisk studie av historieämnets målfrågor i den ryska och sovjetiska skolan 1900-1940.* Stockholm, Universitetsförlaget Dialogos 1987.

KORITZINSKY, T.: *Samfunnsfag og påvirkning. Om samfundsfagenes plass i skolen – og om faglig og ideologisk innhold i læreplaner og lærebøker.* Oslo, Universitetsforlaget 1977.

KRESS, G.: Against arbitrariness: the social production of the sign as a foundational issue in critical discourse analysis. In: *Discourse & Society 4:2,* 1993, pp. 169–193.

LAKOFF, G.: *Women, Fire and Dangerous Things. What Categories Reveal about the Mind.* Chicago, The University of Chicago Press 1987.

van LEEUWEN, T. & S. SELANDER: Picturing "our" heritage in the pedagogic text. Layout and illustrations in an Australian and a Swedish history textbook. Curriculum Studies. (In press, to be published in 1995).

LINDHARDT, J.: *Retorik*. Copenhagen, Munksgaard 1987.

LUNDGREN, U.P. et al. (eds.): *Läroplaner och läromedel*. Stockholm, HLS 1982.

LUNDSTEN, L.G.: *Vem är Tito och vad gör han? Litterär kommunikation i ljuset av filosofisk handlingsteori och Tito Collianders memoarer*. Helsinki, University of Helsinki 1992.

Lysias. Tolv tal. (Bertil Cavallin). Stockholm, Forum 1983.

LÖFDAHL, S.E.: *Fysikämnet i svensk realskola och grundskola. Kartläggning och alternativ ur fysikdidaktisk synvinkel*. (= Uppsala Studies in Education). Stockholm, Almqvist & Wiksell 1987.

MOLANDER, B.: *Räkna rätt och tänka fritt. Rapport från projektet "Utbildning för tillämpning av statistik: Kunskap och kunskapssyn"*. Uppsala, University of Uppsala 1987.

MÅRDSJÖ, K.: *Människa, text, teknik*. Linköping, Affärslitteratur 1992.

NORDKVELLE, Y.: *Bilder av utviklingsland i norske lærebøker*. Oslo, University of Oslo 1987.

NYSTRÖM, B.: *Marcus Fabius Quintilianus. Läroplanskod, läroplan och metodiska anvisningar*. Uppsala, University of Uppsala 1994.

ODHNER, C.T. & K.G. WESTMAN: *Lärobok i fäderneslandets historia för realskolan*. Stockholm, P.A. Norstedts 1930.

OLSSON, L.: *Kulturkunskap i förändring. Kultursynen i svenska geografiläroböcker 1870-1985*. Stockholm, Liber 1986.

POPKEWITZ, T.: *The Formation of the School Subjects. The Struggle for Creating an American Institution*. New York, The Falmer Press 1987.

PRELLI, L. J.: *A Rhetoric of Science*. Columbia, University of South Carolina Press 1989.

POSNER, G.J. et al.: Accomodation of a Scientific Conception: Toward a Theory of Conceptual Change. In: *Science Education 66:2*, 1982, pp. 211-227.

ROKSVOLD, T.: *Retorikk for journalister*. Oslo, J.W. Cappelens Forlag 1991.

Samhällsinsatser på läromedelsområdet. (= SOU 1971:91). Stockholm, Läromedelsutredningen 1971.

SCHOLES, R.: *Textual Power. Literary Theory and the Teaching of English.* New Haven, Yale University Press 1985.

SELANDER, S.: *Textum institutionis. Den pedagogiska väven.* Malmö, CWK Gleerup 1984.

SELANDER, S.: *Lärobokskunskap. Pedagogisk textanalys med exempel från läroböcker i historia 1841–1985.* Lund, Studentlitteratur 1988.

SELANDER, S.: Pedagogiska texter som forskningsfält. In: *Forskning om utbildning 4/1994,* pp. 72-85.

SELANDER, S. & B. ENGLUND (eds.): *Konsten att informera och övertyga. En antologi om pedagogik, text och retorik.* Stockholm, HLS Förlag 1994.

SKYUM-NIELSEN, P.: *Fyndord. Studier i kortformernes retorik.* Copenhagen, Hans Reitzel 1992.

STABERG, E-M.: *Olika världar, skilda värderingar. Hur flickor och pojkar möter högstadiets fysik, kemi och teknik.* Umeå, University of Umeå 1992.

SVENSSON, J.: Den diskursiva texten. In: HOLMBERG, G. & J. SVENSSON (eds.): *Medietexter och medietolkningar.* Lund, Nya Doxa 1995.

TULLY, J.: *Meaning & Context. Quentin Skinner and his Critics.* Cambridge, Polity Press 1989.

WESTBURY, I.: *School Textbooks.* (= Research Report from the Curriculum Laboratory, College of Education 11). Urbana, University of Illinois 1982.

VICKERS, B.: *In Defence of Rhetoric.* Oxford, Clarendon Press 1988.

ÖHMAN, C.: *Historia.* Uppsala, Esselte Studium 1989.

Analyzing Educational Texts

Peder Skyum-Nielsen

Educational texts have a central role in the formation of communities and the education of individuals. It is thus important that producers, teachers and school principals develop a heightened awareness of educational texts and their optimal function.

Such a heightened shared awareness will however only bear weight if there is a consensus about the relevant few concepts and terms. This article will present the overall model and the fundamental ideas which the contributors to this book have agreed in finding useful.

The rhetorical basis

The model is based on the five fundamental factors which occur in any speech or writing situation:

- The speaker   (in Latin "persona")
- The audience   (Latin "auditor")
- The circumstances   ("tempus")
- The theme   ("causa"), and
- The language   ("genus orationis").

Considered in a little more detail, these five factors will be seen as forming **unique connections** in each speech or writing situation. In mathematics lessons with a 6th-grade class one week, the dialogue will be different on Tuesday from on Wednesday. And the same biology book will function very differently for a teacher, depending on which class she is using it with.

The entire interaction around educational texts is a complex one, involving production, selection, distribution and reception, and therefore the group behind this book has not been content with the simple, basic rhetorical model but has expanded it to include no fewer than **thirteen** areas.

The presentation of the analytical model for educational texts is the principal task of the present article. But before proceeding to a consideration of the thirteen areas it may be useful to define a few terms applying to 'the analysis of educational texts'.

Some definitions

First, the very term **"analysis"**: in this book it will be understood as meaning systematic investigations, especially those which resolve the subject into its component parts.

By the term **"text"** is understood a complex of meaning with its own principle of unity, which one or more parties intend to transmit or communicate to (themselves or) others.

Texts can obviously be **verbal**: oral or written. They can also be **para-verbal**: tonal or (purely) musical. Furthermore, texts can also be **non-verbal** – e.g. graphic, visual or iconic ... possibly with separate or serial (moving) pictures.

A maths lesson with any given 6th-grade class can be seen as one text with all these various strata; or it can be regarded as a mainly oral text which also includes written texts produced by publishers and by the pupils themselves.

The maths lesson and the textbook are also examples of the particular kind of texts we are concerned with here: **educational texts**, or texts which have to do with teaching and personal formation.

With this last definition, a framework has been created for analyzing and understanding the texts **in school**. But a number of texts **about** what takes place, and can take place, at school are also regarded as 'educational texts'. Thus a curriculum for the teaching of the mother tongue also satisfies the requirements for being an educational text, as does a ministerial report from 1991 on teaching *Oral presentation*.

It will therefore be found convenient to distinguish between different **levels** of educational texts:

- A text will be at the **zero level** if its content consists of material for actual teaching. In this sense, a literary manual for use in the Gymnasium will be a zero-level educational text, as will a photocopy of a particular poem by Johannes V. Jensen when it is used as a text in (literature) teaching.

– A text will be at the **meta level** if its content **deals with** teaching and education. Gilbert Highet's *The Art of Teaching* (1950) is thus a meta level educational text. The same applies to the curriculum for teaching the mother tongue, and the above-mentioned ministerial report from 1991.

Finally, a third level can be distinguished for the purposes of analysis:
– A text is at the **meta-meta level** if it is a scholarly investigation **of** texts which in their turn deal **with** teaching or education. Examples of such meta-meta texts are the articles in this collection by Vagn Oluf Nielsen and Sten Sjørslev, dealing with curricula.

So far we have defined 'analysis', 'educational' and 'text', and looked at the 'zero', 'meta' and 'meta-meta' levels. Before we proceed to the presentation of the overall model, there remain two terms which have similarly been found useful: 'primary' and 'secondary' educational texts.
– **Primary** educational texts are those which were originally intended to function in education and teaching. Included here are such teaching materials as a series of slides about our food, the 6th-grade mathematics textbook – etc., etc.
– In contrast, **secondary** educational texts are those which can certainly be used in education and teaching, but were not originally intended for that purpose. The aforementioned poem by Johannes V. Jensen is in this category, as is the newspaper leader which is used in the biology lesson because it deals with a relevant topic relating to environmental policies.

"The Thirteen Areas"

The definitions given above have proven useful to the authors of this book when it has been necessary for us to manoeuvre in the very varied landscape of educational texts; but our overall model or "map" has been even more useful.

We have called the model "The Thirteen Areas", because it comprises thirteen groups of circumstances which in our experience frequently repay investigation when analyzing educational texts. Very concisely, these thirteen areas can be summed up in one sentence:

Who says [or understands] **what** to [from] **whom** with **which intention**, in **which medium** and dependent on **which conditions**, at **what time and place** and under the influence of **which teacher persona and teaching method** and controlled by **which formal regulations**, and with **which selection and use of concepts**, with **which verbal and textual practice**, with **which para- and non-verbal communications** ... and with **what overall effect**?

It will be noticed that this condensed formula sets out the fundamental relation between the sender and the receiver of a text, and goes on to elaborate a number of other factors involved in the communication in the order which we have found most natural for the purpose of analysis.

More elaborate ...

Here follows a rather less condensed account of the thirteen areas, with comments:

(1) *Who says [or understands]*

Here the sender, the author, the graphic artist or the producer is determined. – [Or it is the receiver who is determined: the one who understands (reads, hears or sees) the relevant educational text. With the last addition to area (1) we avoid the usually exclusive orientation of our model from the point of view of the sender. This can also be seen in connection with area (3)].

(2) *what*

The second area deals with the content which is communicated via the text: What is its topic? And what attitude or ideology does the text reflect?

(3) *to [from] whom*

Here is the first mention of the addressees, or intended receivers. But there may also be others who actually receive the text. It is worth remembering that as analyst one receives the text in a special manner which is rarely pre-intended. [From the point of view of the receiver, the sender can be determined here, cf. (1)].

(4) *with which intention*

Here the question could also be "why?" What is the intention behind the text? The intention will frequently consist of several parts; and the intention(s) will guide choices within a number of other areas of observation.

(5) *in which medium*

The manifestation of the text is in question here: is it spoken or written? Does it take the form of a book or photocopy, a video, film, cartoon? The distinction between fiction and non-fiction can also be discussed here (cf. Børre Johnsen's article in *Text and Quality*).

(6) *dependent on which conditions*

This area covers the conditions surrounding the production, distribution and consumption of the text: the publishers' frame, printing options, the economy of the market and the production time etc. The purchasing conditions of schools and libraries also belong here. (Cf. Torben Weinreich's and Kurt Hartvig Petersen's articles in this volume).

(7) *at what time and place*

Here the communication is placed in time and space. Under 'space' are also included the institutional, physical, mental and social contexts into which the text enters and in which it is used. The ideological framework of the communication may also be dealt with in detail here. Cf. area (2) above.

(8) *under the influence of which teacher persona and teaching method*

The specific educational context belongs under this area; and it is (8) which determines whether a good, average or poor material functions or appeals at all. (The articles by Karsten Schnack and Else Marie Pedersen give accounts of this).

(9) *controlled by which formal regulations*

In this area belong ministerial orders, teaching guides and curricula, as well as other regulations which control the specific educational text and its use. In Denmark this can apply to both institutional and local, regional and national regulations for the use of teaching material in a given subject.

(10) *with which selection and use of concepts*

What information has been selected for communication? And what is omitted in the text? Which concepts have been selected for transmission by the content of the text? Does this use of concepts harmonise with the linguistic and cognitive development of the receivers?

(11) *with **which verbal and textual practice***

   This is an especially comprehensive area. It includes all the traditional 'observational circumstances' belonging to traditional verbal analysis. In principle it is possible to analyze at one or more segmental levels, from the sentence or period to the chapter and the entire text. The level of comprehensibility and the degree to which the text is adapted to the receiver can be investigated here.

(12) *with **which para- and non-verbal communications***

The para-verbal has to do with the **way** in which the words, the verbal element, are spoken or written. In speech, the para-verbal applies to such matters as articulation, tempo, volume, pitch and tone. In writing it applies to typography, script size, colour, punctuation etc. The whole pictorial and iconic field is reckoned as non-verbal. Music and tonality can be regarded as both para-verbal and non-verbal communications. In this present volume, Marie-Alice Séférian's article deals with the most important interactions between areas (11) and (12).

(13) *with **what overall effect**?*

Here the effect can be described from the point of view of one, several or all the parties involved. There can also be concluding remarks of a special or general nature on the composition of 'the appropriate educational text'. This is the case in several of the articles.

"The Four Pillars"

We will now use a concrete example to flesh out the skeleton of this model. The way the model is put to use can be illustrated by means of a few short texts taken from Peter Weir's acclaimed movie "Dead Poets' Society" 1989. Cf. also the novel *Dead Poets' Society* by N.H. Kleinbaum (New York, Bantam Books 1989).

   At the start of Weir's film, and several times subsequently, four slogans appear on banners: *TRADITION, HONOUR, DISCIPLINE* and *EXCELLENCE*. They are called "The Four Pillars", and they express the fundamental values of the school which is the setting and subject of the film. Let us, **within the fiction of the film** connect "The Four Pillars" with the (beginning of) "The Thirteen Areas":

© MCMLXXXIX Touchstone Pictures. All Rights Reserved.

(1) The **sender** of the slogan text is the school, and the anonymous tradition which derives from the foundation of Welton in 1859. It is received by the boys at the school one hundred years later, in a different age.

(2) The **content** of the slogans is injunctive. The text expresses in concentrated form the bourgeois ideology of industry.

(3) The four key words are said **to the boys** – and the assembled teachers and parents – who together form a great echo chamber for the message to reverberate in. To the parents, the sender is a reassuring institution; for most of the boys, however, it is a kind of monster which is out of touch with 1959, the time of the film.

(4) **The intention** behind the slogan words must be seen as a complex one. In relation to the parents and the outside world, the school wishes to justify its existence. In relation to the teachers and the other staff, the school wishes to create a corporate spirit (which is rejected by Mr. Keating, the teacher who is the film's adult protagonist). As they are presented to the boys, the purpose of the slogans is to discipline and socialise them. For their part, the boys accept the message because they have to. But the distance between the school's official values and the boys' urges becomes too great. And for this reason "The Dead Poets' Society" is revived.

I will now bring this exemplifying analysis to a close and simply maintain that the four key words are manifested in the film as timeless and embroidered in written form on the banners; the words assume a momentary, oral existence when they are recited in chorus, like a prayer, by the whole assembly in the school hall. A further analysis might well elaborate on the way the plot is very rooted in time and place; i.e. with reference to area (7). It would clearly also be pertinent to focus on the influence of the teacher persona under area (8): John Keating versus the rest of the staff.

The effect (13) in this film is of a conflict between systems of norms, between natural urge and compulsion, which results in the main juvenile character (the Neil Perry of the photo) committing suicide.

To the analysis which has merely been suggested here can be added a further one which moves **beyond the fiction of the film**. It is a fact that in the real world a film called "Dead Poets' Society" was made by the director Peter Weir in collaboration with a very wide circle of actors and other film people. In reality, the message on the banners has been **embedded in** the communication between the production team (1) ... and everyone who sees the film (3). The slogans of the fictional world are thus part of the film's (and preceding that, the novel's) overall attitudinal message (2).

The intention (4) of the director, producer and the rest of the team has been firstly to safeguard their own livelihood; but they also wanted to communicate a particular view of human life, schooling and education. This complex intention is manifested in "Dead Poets' Society" by means of the medium of film (5). And thus the entire message from the real world is dependent on the detailed conditions (6) of production, distribution and consumption which applied at the end of the 1980s and have done since then. – Et cetera.

The typical application of the model

It is not usual practice to apply five or six phases of the model as was suggested above. Most users of the model will normally deal with only a few of the thirteen areas at any one time.

I: In a typical analysis of an educational text, the analyst will start by forming an **overall impression** of the object text to ensure that it has been fully grasped and understood.

II: On this basis, the analyst can then formulate or reformulate his/her **purpose** in examining the text more closely.

III: Following this, the analyst may become especially interested in two or three areas, which will thus be **selected for closer investigation**. These may for instance be the structure and order of information in a series of geographical slides (areas 10 and 11); or the print quality and typography of the various features in a physics book for the 9th grade (area 12); or the sales conditions in the 1990s of a CD-ROM course in correct English for adults (area 6). And so on.

IV: As a fourth stage the analyst will typically go on to a **(detailed) analysis** of the area(s) selected: e.g. structure; typography; or sales conditions.

V: Finally, the analyst may draw conclusions from the analysis, either independently or in collaboration with others, and may thus be able to contribute to **the improvement** of various aspects of the type or genre of 'educational text' in question.

This has been the procedure used by the authors of the articles in this book: they have dealt with a variety of educational texts and a wide selection of their interesting aspects.

Other applications

The reader of this book can therefore use the model to gain an impression of how the articles in *Text and Quality* are distributed on the map which has now been drawn of the landscape of educational texts.

It can also be helpful for readers to use this map or model to locate their **own interests** within teaching and research. "The Thirteen Areas" were used for this purpose at the Second International Conference on the analysis of educational texts (Joensuu, Finland, 1993).

And readers might perhaps want to locate on the map some of the **criteria and parameters of quality** which are most significant for them. Teachers, text producers, reviewers, librarians, administrators and students may all find some of their most important quality parameters in the following list:

(1) Sender, author, producer:
  • The sender's competence and knowledge (logos)?
  • The sender's commitment and wellbeing (pathos)?
  • The sender's general credibility (ethos)?
(2) Content, attitude, ideology:
  • Does the text deal with its topic in an all-round manner?
  • Does the text have a precise and lively content? Humour?
  • What is its entertainment value?
  • What explicitly is the educational and ideological foundation?
(3) The addressees; the intended and actual receivers:
  • Has the text any clear target group(s)?
  • What degree of commitment and expertise do the receivers have?
  • Is the text addressed clearly? Has it a clear "you-point"?
  • Does the text offer its addressees suitable challenges?
(4) The intention:
  • Has the text a clear (complex of) intention(s)?
  • Does the praxis of the text correspond to its (declared or interpreted) intention(s)?
(5) The medium; fact – faction – fiction; genre:
  • Is the medium chosen appropriately?
  • Does the text operate in a clearly factual or fictional manner? Does it have authenticity?
  • Does the text represent an appropriate selection of material? Of facts?
  • Are the conventions of the genre used fully? Is there genre innovation or mixing?
(6) The conditions of production, distribution and consumption:
  • Low costs and a reasonable profit for the producer?
  • Low costs and a reasonable profit for the distributor?
  • Low price and good value for the consumer?
  • How durable is the textual product?
(7) Time, context, place:
  • Is the content up-to-date?
  • Is it suitably adapted to the situation and context of use?
(8) The teacher persona, the teaching method:
  • Does the text guide the teacher through the teaching?
  • Does the text give the teacher sufficient freedom?

- Are the fundamental ideas of the text and the teacher in agreement with each other?

(9) Control by formal regulations:
- Does the text conform to the regulations currently – or previously – in force, for instance for the aim and content of the teaching?

(10) Composition, selection and use of concepts?
- Has the text a logical and well-arranged macrostructure? Does it proceed in an interesting and appropriate manner?
- Is the text transparent in its microstructures?
- Does the text contain clear definitions?
- Is the progression of the textual (educational) material appropriate?
- Is there an appropriate selection of concepts?
- Are there vivid examples?
- Is there a suitable amount of exercises?
- Are there an index and a table of contents?

(11) The verbal and textual praxis:
- Has the text special literary and stylistic qualities?
- Has it a personal tone and expository form?
- How well are textual coherence and cohesion achieved?
- What are the oral qualities? (N.B.: These can also be found in written texts).
- Is there a sufficient degree of verbal comprehensibility? Of readability?
- Is the language precise and correct?
- Are there striking images? And pithy key passages?
- Is the exposition sufficiently objective?

(12) Physical appearance; para- and non-verbal messages:
- Is the physical appearance of the text suitable? (Format, durability, attractiveness, quality of materials).
- Are the pictures sharp and well reproduced? Are there enough illustrations?
- Interaction between text and pictures?
- Appropriate typography and layout?

(13) The total effect of the text:
- In relation to the producer ... distributor ... receiver and consumer?

- Considerations of the composition and function of future related educational texts?

Readers can reduce, change or add to this overview as needed, thereby creating their own models. What is vital is that we develop and improve the contemporary conception of 'the good educational text', and that as far as possible we establish a consensus.

Postmodern conclusion

The fundamental concept of the text has by no means remained static during the years that I have worked on textual production and analysis. And now it looks as if we adults are facing entirely new problems when we attempt to teach the present generation of young people about our way of understanding texts.

Visual media like music videos and commercials accustom the young to texts whose pace and mixed forms were unknown in the past. (Cf. the above article by Susanne V. Knudsen and Birgitte Tufte).

Previously, a novel was a novel, a short story was a short story, and the textbook was really a book. That is to say, texts were seen as "monolevel"; but the media developments which have occurred during the last decade have given the young a new, "multilevel" conception of the text.

How should we, the "monolevel" teachers, producers and researchers, relate to this new generational difference?

Index

Jørgen Olesen

DATE DUE

DEMCO, INC. 38-2971

Lewis and Clark College - Watzek Library

3 5209 00615 9152